Published by
Jack Petchey Foundation
Exchange House
13-14 Clements Court
Clements Lane
Ilford
Essex IG1 2QY
Tel: 020 8252 8000
www.jackpetcheyfoundation.org.uk

First published in Great Britain 2006.

Hardback ISBN (978-0-9576816-0-6).

Printed and bound in Great Britain by
Elle Media Group
Seax Way
Southfields Industrial Park
Basildon, Essex
SS15 6SW
Tel: 01268 413611
Fax: 01268 541637
www.ellemediagroup.co.uk

50/50 MAN

The Jack Petchey Story

by Jack Petchey with Andy Staines

Best wishes!

Jack Petchey

~ *Acknowledgements* ~

I have written this book for my family - my grandchildren, and perhaps even their grandchildren, should they be interested in their roots.

My thanks go to everyone who has made this book possible - my family, my friends, my mentors, my loyal staff - without them, I would not be as successful and happy as I am.

Particular thanks to my secretary, Barbara, whose painstaking work over the years in preparing this book has probably left her knowing me almost as well as I do myself!.....well nearly!

My deep appreciation also goes to my Mother, without whose love and support in my early years, I may never have had the impetus to "make things work".

~ CONTENTS ~

~ *Introduction* ~

Why write my story? It's a question I've asked frequently of late. My friends, staff and family have all felt the brunt of my bombardment. Who'll read it? Will it be any good? Will it sell? *Should* it sell? With varying opinions I've listened to all the answers and they have made me realise something - it's not really my place to say; for the first time in my career I've come to the conclusion that these decisions are simply not mine to make. Judgement of this book rests with you - the readers. It's down to you now, I can only put pen to paper and leave my story with you.

So - where to start? After eighty eight years I have a lot of memories to delve through.

I'll begin with a tale that I often recall for the guests at my charity presentations - more of which later - and one that tells of my first real lesson in marketing and one that may have even shaped my life.

In 1937 at the age of eleven I had found work in the greengrocers on the corner of High Street North, in Manor Park, East London, for a man named George Lawrence, who was quite a character to say the least. He asked me to separate a batch of tomatoes - polishing one half and displaying them in separate stacks. I was told 'one half at the low price, the other at the high price'. Instantly questioning as to why, George replied with a comment that has stayed with me ever since - 'Some like 'em cheap, some like 'em expensive'. In other words - some people like a bargain while others like "the best". In hindsight, I see this as my first real lesson in marketing.

By the age of twelve I had learned many similar lessons from George and was working all the hours I could. However, one day I found myself learning a lesson of a completely different nature, in front of a Judge. I had been delivering a bag of the aforementioned tomatoes, to a customer in Shelley Avenue, and was caught red handed by a member of the School Board. Both George and my parents were hauled before the local magistrates for me working under age. Having been caught with all the evidence, it seemed like a bullet-proof case against me - and my employer. However, fate dealt its own twist. The summons, which stated that I was delivering **vegetables,** was dismissed when the Bench agreed with my solicitor that - as we all well know - tomatoes are, in fact, a *fruit!*

I may well have got away on a technicality, but as far as court cases go, this stood me in very good stead for the future.

*If you think you can't
- you CAN'T....*

*If you think you can,
you CAN!*

Chapter One

An East End Upbringing

~ *Chapter One* ~

An East End Upbringing.

Born to parents Stanley and Dorothy on 19th July 1925, I was third in the family line. My brother Douglas, the eldest, died of appendicitis when he was six years old leaving my two-year older sister Joan as my only sibling.

At this time the family lived in Settle Road, London E13. Although I remember very little, I do know that Settle Road runs alongside Plaistow Station and that my mother's parents had a sweetshop there.

The place I remember as my first real home was on Stanley Road - No 7, in Manor Park, London E12. My parents had rented a flat on the ground floor of a small terraced house, like many in that part of London, which consisted of one room separated with folding wooden doors. The entire living space, if you can call it that, was no bigger than 10' x 12' - not very big for a four strong family in 1928. We had an outside toilet, and our tin bath hung on the fence in the garden and was carried into the kitchen every Friday evening, filled with hot water from the copper, and we all bathed in it – eldest down to youngest! To our standards nowadays, this sounds quite archaic and unhygienic, but it was considered quite normal then. No central heating then either – I

My Mother Dorothy (Doll) Irene Petchey (Cubbon) (1904-1971) outside my Grand-parents' shop in Plaistow

Grand-mother & Mother Emma Petchey (1861-1943)

Father, Stanley James Petchey (1900-1946)

vividly remember my Dad sitting in the kitchen and constantly berating us kids for running in and out and letting all the cold air inside. Probably if we had to worry about the coal bills, we would have been a little bit more considerate, but no doubt that was the last thing on our minds. I've often said that I had a hard upbringing, but looking back it was no harder than anyone else in those days. We all made the best of what we had, which wasn't a lot. We didn't think of ourselves as 'poor', but we knew we weren't 'rich'.

My sister Joan will recall, as I do, being sent to afternoon Sunday School at the Baptist Church on Barclay Road. Looking back with much wiser eyes I see now that this was when my parents got to spend some 'quality time' together alone in such a small space.

After Stanley Road we found ourselves at 56 Goldsmith Avenue, Manor Park – in a flat next to Arnopps Garage, where my father (known as Happy Jack) worked and where I would wash down cars in the yard. It was in that yard at a very early age that I drove my first car and got to grips with the basics of gear selection, clutch control and so forth. Incidentally, Arnopps was the place where I would first dream with a friend, Ken Crispin, about running a high class car service with drivers in smart uniforms that opened the door and greeted customers appropriately.

Our first real 'house' of our own was only a few doors from the current one, at No 48, rented for the princely sum of £1.25 a week - I remember thinking at the time that we had 'arrived'. However we did have to take in a lodger called 'Goggles' (he wore glasses) to pay the rent. A date that stands out from this time is 17th October 1935, the day I passed my 'Tenderpad' test with the 14th East Ham Scout Pack. My 'Tenderfoot' Badge came later in June of 1937. As a very keen Scout I attended monthly Sunday church parades in High Street North, on the corner of Strone Road, marching through the streets, proud as punch, with my Mother Doll looking on – even prouder.

Nowadays when I attend presentations for the Jack Petchey Foundation and see the youngsters in their uniforms, proudly displaying their Achievement Award certificates & medallions, the memories of my time in the Scouts come flooding back. I never fail to smile when recalling my troop leader and his girlfriend trying to sing.

The Scouting organisation is one of which I am very fond; in the early days of business I was heavily involved in helping out the handicapped scouts and would, later in life, be presented with the highest ever civilian Scouting award, the 'Thank You' badge at Baden Powell House in London - at the time I felt as proud as I did in my days with the East Ham 14th. Since then I have been awarded two further accolades, the "Silver Acorn" and the "Silver

THE
BOY SCOUTS' ASSOCIATION.

EAST HAM & BARKING DISTRICT.

We certify that

Jack Petchy _____ of the

14th East Ham (BP) Group

has qualified for the TENDERFOOT BADGE.

L. Jones _____ Scoutmaster

J. Hodge _____ Registrar

Registered Number. **302**

Date *14. 6. 37*

EAST HAM & BARKING BOY SCOUTS'
LOCAL ASSOCIATION.

WOLF CUB SECTION.

We certify that Cub *Jack Petchy*

of the *14th East Ham* Pack

has passed the TENDERPAD test.

A. C. Hayes act'g CM. Examiner.

D. Thackray Registrar.

Date *17. 10. 35* Registered Number **102**

Boy Scouts Memorabilia

Essex Road School

The young Petcheys c 1930

Wolf". I think it is safe to say that the Scouts helped shape my life and I am very proud that through the Jack Petchey Foundation I have been fortunate enough to enjoy a very rewarding relationship with such an admirable organisation.

At the top of Goldsmith Avenue was an Ironmongers shop in which I worked lunchtimes and evenings, as well as pushing a tricycle around the streets delivering cans of paraffin and bundles of firewood. During the lunch hours, particularly on Mondays, I would serve a penny's worth of mustard pickles, loose out of large jars, to one customer, to the next a handful of powdered distemper (white powder commonly used for decorating at the time) – the next would want 4 pickled onions, the next a loose pound of washing soda – and so it went on, I certainly never ever remember washing my hands.

Occasionally my cousin Ron Johnson would assist in the shop. One day we were curious to discover what the shop manager was up to in the back wallpaper storage room. Peering through the keyhole I saw him canoodling with one of the lady customers. Ron was down in the basement, where two boards had been placed on the steps for sliding packages down. The manager moved away from the girl – I assumed (rightly) that he was heading my way; I jumped quickly on to the boards and slid gracefully into the basement before he reached the top of the stairs. He accused me (rightly) of spying through the keyhole, but by a stroke of good fortune

Ron stood by me, swearing blind that I had never left the basement and saving me a good hiding in the process.

At two years my senior, Ron also worked for a man by the name of Charlie Bolton in Chesterfield Road, Manor Park, delivering early morning papers – he put a word in and got me a job working for Charlie – firstly the 6am delivery round – after Charlie had marked up the papers on his kitchen table - and then pushing his pram, loaded with papers to his stand at East Ham Station. I'd also collect the paper bill money from his customers on a Saturday, trailing round the streets to each and every house.

It wasn't all work; it was quite common to find us kids playing tricks in the street. For example, we would put a milk bottle on a wall with string tied to it, waiting until some poor soul walked past and scare the wits out of them by pulling on the string and smashing the bottle to the ground.

Another occasion found my sister Joan inside the house at 48 - we tied a piece of string to the door knocker, hid in the garden across the road and repeatedly pulled on the string. Joan kept answering the door and finding nobody there naturally got scared, so much so that she dashed through the hole in the back garden fence to Mr Fox at number 50. With his son Clifford, Mr Fox fell foul of the joke as we repeated what we did with Joan. This was extremely amusing to the both of us, until of course

**Douglas Stanley Petchey
(1922-1928)**

Sister Joan & myself, with Sally

we were caught and severely scolded.

Another of my favourite pranks with Ron was to sit in the front garden, just behind the privet hedge when it was dark, wait for someone to pass and drop a coin - then spend the next ten minutes trying to suppress fits of laughter as they scrabbled around on the ground looking for the coin they thought they heard drop.

Ron and I certainly got into some scrapes together and one left our mothers literally crying over spilt milk! Milk was sold by a street trader, who wheeled a barrow carrying a large churn from which the housewives would fill their jugs. One day, out of devilment, I turned the tap on and let all the milk spill out onto the road. There was, of course, quite a commotion when the milkman found out – and I loudly protested my innocence and blamed my cousin, Ron! Our two mothers fell out and mine ended up paying for all the wasted milk. Was I ashamed of myself? No – to me it was a real prank – and Ron obviously forgave me as we remained lifelong friends!

During these good times I remember being sent down to the local shop to buy three cigarettes for a penny, for my mother and her friend, Mrs McEwan, who would share them, one each and the other would be snapped in half. My friend Ginger Barrow also bought cigarettes from the same place and could be found smoking them down the alley at the top of Goldsmith Avenue.

Saturday mornings were spent working for Millens the Butcher, who had a big old-fashioned bicycle, with a deep basket on the front. I would ride over to Wanstead Park Avenue – in those days considered to be very posh – all the 'nobs' had residences there – to deliver meat. Being as big as the bike was and being as small as I was, the bike fell over on one occasion tipping meat into the road - I simply picked it up, re-wrapped and delivered it – no questions asked! It's amazing to think what we could get away with in those days.

One of the obvious perks of having a job came when I purchased my first bicycle. Back then it was big deal to me, for the first time in my life I'd have something that was mine that I had earned. It was a three gear racing model and cost me 65 shillings from Saxby's on High Street North. Taking no guarantees, due to knowing me from the hardware shop opposite, they accepted weekly instalments. I was so proud that I never failed once to make a payment on the one thing that was truly mine.

I have very fond memories of my time at Goldsmith Avenue, as well as fond memories of the people there too. My friend 'Ginger Barrow' lived at number 4 – and I would often be invited to his house for tea. I don't know why, but I was always surprised that his father – a Chief Petty Gunnery Officer based at Greenwich Naval College, used to preside over the table and pick out the little plugs from inside the winkles! This was usually the job we kids used to do at home – Bibby, the Fishmonger, would sell winkles from his two wheeled barrow in the road, and it would be up to Joan and I to pick out the winkle plugs with a pin – we then went on to stick these little plugs all over our faces – which, of course, we found hilarious at the time.

Another family I remember well were the Rouse's from No. 23. My sister Joan helped deliver their baby Douglas in 1956. After giving birth twice herself, Joan still admits that this was the most amazing thing she had ever seen!

In fact over the years not only the father, Ron Rouse Senior – a real "Jack of All Trades" - but many of the children, ten in total – would work for me. Two, to this day, remain in my employment.

In between my various part time jobs came school, first at Essex Road, Manor Park then on to Monega Road Senior School, at age 11. I was a poor student with little interest in learning, never doing homework nor receiving the encouragement to do it. I never owned a book, encyclopaedia or map, and was bottom in most subjects. If you asked me today about the merits of schooling I'd tell you that it is essential, especially in the age of computers and high tech wizardry, but in those days if you had the right will and mindset I felt that you didn't really need it.

Joan on the other hand was a very conscientious scholar – she went to secondary school and fared much better than I. Known to be a better student she went on to earn the qualifications

I now recommend be acquired.

My Grandparents lived in Libra Road Plaistow. With Cousin Ron I would visit at weekends, we would thoroughly enjoy the train ride over. On Saturday nights we would go to the top of Plaistow High Road for faggots and pease pudding, someone in the family would go round the corner for a quart jug of beer and we would have 'sippers' on the way back home from the off-license. When the drinking got high and company too excited, my mother and father would miss the train from Plaistow and I would spend the hour's walk home perched on my father's shoulders. On a Sunday, we knew that the Ticket Office at West Ham Station was closed, so we would simply buy a platform ticket for a penny at Plaistow Station, ride the train to

Grandma Emma & Grandpa James Petchey

West Ham, slip under the barrier, then walk over the footbridge to the opposite platform, ride back to Plaistow, and simply show our platform ticket to get through the barrier. Cheating, I know, but great fun!

Grandfather Jim was a signalman on the London Midlands Scottish Railway (LMS) working a signal box just outside Bromley-by-Bow Station. On odd occasions we were allowed to visit him at work, wondering at the highly polished large brass levers, the little box on the wall and a constantly ringing telephone. I always recall how spick and span he kept it, always very proud of his work. I'm sure that through people like Grandfather Jim I learned the work ethic that would eventually get me to where I am today.

Brewing his own wine (which he kept in the cupboard under the stairs) was one of Granddad Jim's true loves, as well as great fondness for drinking it. Another was cricket and by all accounts he was quite good at it, except on the one occasion that he took me, he was out on his first ball – I don't remember ever going again!

Both Joan and I have very fond memories of our Grandfather, with clear recollections of the handful of copper coins he would give us when we visited, which we would spend on Nestlé chocolate bars from the vending machine at Plaistow station.

Somewhere around 1935 I have distinct memories of the Country Holiday Fund. At school there was a programme where children whose parents were unable to afford a holiday could travel to the countryside for two weeks. Travelling by rail with a group of other children from the programme I

arrived at a station - the name of which escapes me –
to be greeted by my temporary 'foster parents' for the
fortnight. Upon arrival at my allotted billet, I found
that it was a very poor home – far poorer than the
one I came from! The house was in a terrible state of
disrepair and I clearly recollect orange boxes being
used as dining chairs around a rickety old table. I left
the house on the pretext of posting a letter home and
was later found by a passer-by crying on my way to
the station, with the intention of going home.
Looking back I'm sure I was just homesick. Anyway I
was left in the custody of the local organiser for the
programme, taken to her home – a palace by the
standards I had just come from – and there I stayed
to the end of my holiday. What a result!

All ready for my holiday!

By July 1939 I'd left Monega Road School and started work as an office boy at the Solicitors Law Stationary Society in Fetter Lane. However this being 1939 meant that not only did my life change in a business sense, it changed - as everyone else's did - with the outbreak of World War Two.

He who never fell -
never climbed!

Chapter Two.

The War Years

~ *Chapter Two* ~

The War Years

"I'm speaking to you from the Cabinet Room at 10 Downing Street. This morning the British Ambassador in Berlin handed the German Government a final note stating that, unless we hear from them by 11 o'clock that they were prepared at once to withdraw their troops from Poland, a state of war would exist between us. I have to tell you now that no such undertaking has been received, and that consequently this country is at war with Germany.

Now may God bless you all. May He defend the right. For it is evil things that we shall be fighting against - brute force, bad faith, injustice, oppression and persecution - and against them I am certain that right will prevail."

Neville Chamberlain

11am, 3rd September 1939.

My family, just as most others in the country, were huddled around the wireless amid fine tuning and calls for silence, when the then Prime Minister, Neville Chamberlain, spoke those now historically significant words. My mother and the other adults were in tears at the prospect but being a 'gung ho' kid it didn't really sink in - the severity of it all would hit me at a later date.

Being a Boy Scout I was enlisted as a Police Messenger. With my friend Ginger Barrow I was to report for duty to East Ham Police Station, in full Scout uniform and a white armband. I left home on my bicycle, rode across the tram-lines in the High Street to the Police Station and reported for my first war duty. Quite an adventure I thought! I served as a messenger until the age of 16, at which time I was old enough to ride a motorcycle and get a licence. I then transferred to being a messenger boy in the AFS (Auxiliary Fire Service), while my cousin Ron was a motorcycle messenger for the Home Guard.

We - Ginger Barrow and I - served for some 4 years; right through the height of the war, the bombings and the Blitz, in fact there was an unexploded bomb outside Number 44 Goldsmith Avenue. We had to walk past it for a few days until the Bomb Disposal Unit came to defuse it. Were we scared? No, more curious than anything else.

During the Blitz some of the houses in Goldsmith Avenue - Numbers 90 to 100 - were destroyed, killing many people - one of which was my school girlfriend Eileen Saunders; a very sad day, which suddenly brought the real horror of war home to me.

Another good friend at the time was Dick Beasley - who lived in Kensington Avenue, also in Manor Park. We were great cyclists and could always be seen on our bikes. Dick started off as a baker's boy, and went on to bake in the Merchant

One of the loyal band of
Police Messengers

16 years old

Navy, where he was torpedoed no less than three times. He eventually went on to marry a girl from the Land Army named Violet.

While my mother and big sister Joan lived and often slept in the Anderson Shelter in the garden of Number 48 during the Blitz, I split my time between the Police Station in East Ham, The Fire Station at the Catholic Church in Church Road and the Auxiliary Fire Station in Salisbury Road, Manor Park Broadway. Never a dull moment for me! No doubt Joan was scared stiff, particularly when she was expecting her first child, Jill, and she had to dash from the shelter to the house to give birth in between bombing raids!

Ginger Barrow was as close a friend as one could have in those days. As I mentioned before, he lived at Number 4 Goldsmith Avenue and we were always on duty together, had great respect for each other's families and were often to be found in each other's houses. He went on to marry my cousin, Betty Johnson.

By the age of seventeen it was inevitable that I would be 'called up' so I decided what I was going to do and volunteered for the Royal Navy. I was called up on 9th August 1943 to join the training ship HMS Collingwood at Fareham near Portsmouth. The morning I was to report for service, my mother was in tears. 'Don't go with those nasty women, will you Jack?' she wept as I left the house with my father - who had also served in the Navy

We were an energetic bunch!

many years before - who walked me up Goldsmith
Avenue, shaking my hand for the very first time, as
off I went with some trepidation to 'join the Navy
and win the war!'

For some unknown reason I was selected to be
an Officer Training Recruit, its most distinguishing
feature was having to wear a white armband to
identify us from the others. After three months of
the training I failed the selection process and
remember feeling rather upset and slightly cheated. I
felt at the time that one of my competitors - who
was educated at Eton - qualified above me and I
thought this to be wrong as this man displayed no
'zip' or 'vigour' and seemed to lack all leadership
skills necessary to be an officer, while I was left

*Ron Johnson, Jack Petchey
& friend, Ronnie Loder*

*Myself as a young
Naval Cadet*

behind feeling like a failure. I complained but it was a futile attempt as I was posted to the Fleet Air Arm. I realise now that I was nowhere near 'officer material' but still felt somewhat hurt to be selected initially, have my hopes raised, only to have them dashed later and it came as something of a crushing blow to my ego.

Electrical Air Fitter was the position I was granted upon joining the Fleet Air Arm. Attending the many courses my mathematics improved and I learned a great deal about management. I threw myself into it, passed my mathematics examinations and finished up as a Petty Officer.

The war was at its peak and the Royal Air Force was in desperate need of aircraft engineers. I was sent to the Air Force and stationed at an RAF aerodrome in Dunmow, Essex. I was predominantly working on Sterlings and Halifax Bombers by the time D-Day arrived on 6th June 1944, and we were responsible for the service of the aircraft assisting the liberation of France from the occupying Germans during the Normandy landings. It was terrifying at times but made you grow up fast and separated the mice from the men.

My first duty at Dunmow was Duty Electrician on the far side of the airfield. At 10 o'clock at night, in the pouring rain, I was taken to a hut to sit by myself and ensure the beacon for incoming aircraft was operational. I remember vividly being scared of the dark and being alone. So frightened, in fact, that

I took to the iron bed in the corner, fell asleep, and I was totally unaware that the Duty Officer was trying to contact me by phone. The officer and a woman WRAF driver came over to the hut. With the instinct acquired in Naval training I leapt to attention - unfortunately minus my trousers! Naval discipline should have dictated that I be locked up for six months but the Air Force Officer simply looked at me and said: 'Keep awake lad, keep awake.'

Another typical wartime night found me travelling back to Dunmow during the blackout. Every street light was dead, no light emitted from the windows of the houses, everyone obeying the rules and blocking any light from seeping out. It was total darkness - nothing but moonlight. Thinking my motorbike was running out of petrol, it came to a stop. In an act of amazing stupidity on my part, I removed the petrol cap and lit a match to check the fuel level! It doesn't take a genius to work out what happened next - BANG - on my toes I ran up the road to avoid the flames. Then it hit me 'that's my only motorbike'. I ran back, fanned the flames and pushed it back to the base, which, incidentally, was quite a long way - just payment for my lack of common sense, I suppose.

Any man that served in the forces in those days - or these for that matter - will tell you that you have to stand up for yourself. Each morning at 6 am, armed with a cup, we would make our way to the mess and help ourselves to cocoa from a big barrel, having to beat away cockroaches first. Without fail a big man by the name of Lou Wade would nudge my arm, causing me to spill my cocoa - to laughter all round. Eventually becoming sick of this, I told him in no uncertain terms that if he persisted he would soon be wearing the cocoa. With confident arrogance, and in front of a mess full of sailors looking on, he stepped over and nudged me hard again, leaving me no other choice than to make good my threat, throwing cocoa over his uniform. Not being allowed to fight didn't stop him from challenging me to one in the gym that evening, which I accepted with great fear and trepidation. I got to the gym expecting to be ripped to pieces, only to find Wade wasn't there! Relieved that I had escaped this fate, it taught me to stand up for myself or the Lou Wades of the world will turn up.

As a real treat - and at great sacrifice - my mother, even with the hindrance of rations, would bake, and send to the base, a fruitcake, and I in turn would send home shirts, socks and blankets. On one occasion I had bought some warm blankets from the 'slops' (Naval slang for the store) with the intention of sending them home. I went to the next hut to borrow string to tie up the parcel only to discover on my return that the blankets were gone, stolen in the blink of an eye. My complaint to the Master-at-Arms fell on deaf ears, his reply being 'It's only since you war reserves have come in that we've had this stealing problem.' In my ignorance I responded

HMS Collingwood

'My father says its only criminals, people out of work and those unhappy at home who join the Navy.' Thank goodness the Master-at-Arms had a sense of humour.

Whilst washing at a sink in the barracks, my back 'went' and I finished up in a small building that was doubling up as a hospital ward. I was left totally on my own, I didn't see a soul from the moment I arrived. My need to visit the toilet got greater and greater, so with much difficulty I crept out of the door and into the toilet. Of course while I was in there, the ward orderly came into my room, saw that I was out of bed and reported me for malingering! Needless to say I got no help or treatment after that - just my luck.

My Sister Joan gave birth to my nephew, Michael Bateman, in 1944, in Birmingham, where she had gone to stay with relatives to escape the London bombing raids. I had been on a short electrical engineering course at Ashden-under-Lyme, and was travelling down to London the next day, so called in to see my new born nephew. The train home, I recall, was packed full of soldiers and servicemen like myself, shoulder to shoulder both in the corridors and carriages, with their bags slung about everywhere, causing great confusion and annoyance to the ticket inspectors who couldn't get through to check the tickets - or vouchers as they were in those days. The train approached Euston at a very slow speed, and we were greeted by incoming

Doodlebugs, causing me to take cover in the common instinctive way - that is, diving for cover. Like anyone else who witnessed the Doodlebugs, I can clearly recall the terrible sound they would make and then the engine would cut out shortly before finding their target. These mechanised, pilotless bombs could be heard in the air, but when you heard the engine die you knew it was time to duck. The Germans sent more than 2,500 Doodlebugs - killing some 5,000 Londoners.

When I look back at the black and white film reels and photos of wartime I see a dark and gloomy world, but I certainly don't remember it like that. To me it was full of colour and despite the dire situation it was also full of hope, laughter and comradeship. If anything, the war brought people together rather than tear them apart. I now see something as simple as whistling playing its part in keeping up peoples' spirits. People whistled a lot in those days - something you don't often hear now.

The end of the war is a hard thing to describe - the feeling of elation and relief were only two of the many emotions felt by the country when Japan finally surrendered and put an end to the fighting. It would be a time of change for everyone, me especially, as I now had to decide what to do with my life.

If a copy of this Form is required,
Form S. 1243 is to be used.

S.—459 (Revised—August, 1939).

CERTIFICATE of the Service of

SURNAME (In Block Letters)	CHRISTIAN NAME OR NAMES
PETCHEY	Jack

in the Royal Navy.

NOTE.—The corner of this certificate is to be cut off where indicated if the man is discharged with a "Bad" character or with disgrace, or if specially directed by the Admiralty. If the corner is cut off, the fact is to be noted in the Ledger.

Port Division

Official No.

Date of Birth

Where born { Town or Village / County

Trade or occupation on entry

Religious Denomination — Church of England

Man's Signature on discharge to Pension

Nearest known Relative or Friend.
(To be noted in pencil.)

Relationship : MOTHER

Name : DOROTHY IRENE

Address : 48, GOLDSMITH AVE.
MANOR PARK
LONDON E12

All Engagements, including Non-C.S., to be noted in these Columns.

Date of actually volunteering	Commencement of time	Period volunteered for
1.		
2.		
3.		
4.		
5.		
6.		

Swimming Qualifications.

Date.	Qualification.	Signature.
1.		
2.		
3.		
4.		
5.		
6.		

Medals, Clasps, &c., L.S. and G.C. Gratuity. (see also Page 4).

Date received or forfeited	Nature of Decoration	Date received or forfeited	Nature of Decoration
22.11.66			

Description of Person	Stature		Chest, In.	Colour of			Marks, Wounds, and Scars
	Feet	In.		Hair	Eyes	Complexion	
On Entry as a Boy							
On advancement to man's rating, or on entry under 25 years							
On re-engagement or re-entry for C.S. or for Non-C.S. after attaining 28 years							
Further description if necessary							

CAUTION : This is an Official document. Any alteration made to it without proper authority,

Record from the Fleet Air Arm

Four Steps to Achievement

- **PLAN** *purposefully.*
- **PREPARE** *prayerfully.*
- **PROCEED** *positively.*
- **PURSUE** *persistently.*

Chapter Three

Not Management Material

~ *Chapter Three* ~

"Not Management Material"

Upon returning to civilian life, having been discharged from the Fleet Air Arm, it was customary to return to one's former place of employment. So on 17th January 1947, I made the decision not to stay on as a Petty Officer in the Fleet Air Arm and return to the Solicitors Law Stationery Society.

However, I soon came to the conclusion that life in an accounts department, after serving an active one, was difficult, proving mundane and lacking the excitement of service and comradeship of my Fleet Air Arm colleagues.

Back to 22 Chancery Lane then, to work with legal forms, books, stationery, and other general items. For a short time I assisted a Mr Collingwood, the Sales Representative, and looked after the needs of the Law Society on the other side of Chancery Lane. I learned another of my life altering lessons from Mr Collingwood: How To Get Things Done. During the early part of the post-war era there was a tremendous shortage of items everywhere, including the stationery world, and in particular the Legal profession, where there was a scarcity of pink tape that was used to tie 'briefs' up with. It was clearly

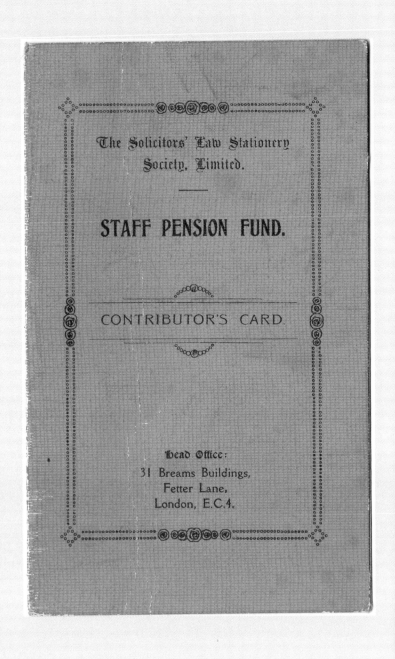

The Solicitors' Law Stationery
Society, Limited.

—

STAFF PENSION FUND.

CONTRIBUTOR'S CARD.

Head Office:
31 Breams Buildings,
Fetter Lane,
London, E.C.4.

very necessary to look after the Law Society, being our best customer, and one of my main duties was to ensure that they had all their requirements met - however the shortage meant that I failed to do this - leaving me to explain in desperation to Mr Collingwood that this item was simply *not* available. As was becoming customary, I came in the next day to find the much needed item on my desk, to which Mr Collingwood would say 'Do try son, *do try*' and it was from him that I would learn that nothing is impossible - the impossible just needs that extra effort!

I recently made contact with someone, David Luff, who worked as Office Junior and he reminded me of the times we would go out at lunch-times - stare up at the sky, as if we could see something - and before long a crowd of people would gather, all trying to see what *we* could see. After a while we were moved on by the police - we thought it was a great laugh!

The new, so-called, progressive thinking of the time dictated that companies had Personnel Officers and the SLSS were no exception. Once appointed, the Personnel Officer made it known that anyone who wished to be considered for management could make a formal application and sit a test. I was *absolutely certain* at this point in my life that I wanted to be a manager and duly applied with eager anticipation. With the test taken it was just a case of waiting for the verdict, which came when I was

This is to Certify *that*

Mr. *J. Peterby*

of *48. Goldsmith Avenue, E.12*

became a *Full* rate Contributor to the Society's

Pension Fund on the *19th July*

19 *41*

Department or Branch *Counting House*

Date of Birth *19. 7. 25.* Admitted *28. 7. 41.*

Pension Service Commenced *19th July 1941.*

Date *20th August 1941.*

A. J. Mansfield

Secretary.

This Card must be surrendered when
application is made for any benefit
or for the return of Contributions.

Every benefit under the Scheme is strictly personal, and any attempt to assign or raise money on a benefit renders it liable to forfeiture. (See Rule 21.)

Any Death Benefit payable, if £75 or less, will be paid to the person in whose favour a form of nomination has been accepted by the Managing Trustees or, in the absence of nomination, to such person as the Managing Trustees think fit. Where the Death Benefit is over £75, representation of the Estate must be taken out, and either Probate of the Will or Letters of Administration produced to the Secretary, from whom further information can be obtained. (See Rule 18.)

Well, I'm glad I've got a pension to look forward to!

called before the Personnel Officer who informed me that, in his opinion, I was *not* management material. After suffering such indignity I promptly handed in my notice and left the company.

Some consolation came when Mr Holroyd, the Managing Director, called me into his office to explain that there had been a misunderstanding - but my dignity had suffered badly and I felt that I simply could not work for a company that showed such a lack of confidence in me.

So now I found myself with no income and in desperate need of it at home! My mother would need her housekeeping! What could I do? I took £60 (my entire life's worth at the time) and bought an Armstrong Siddeley motorcar. A little "wet behind the ears" I looked over and purchased this car in a dimly lit garage only to find upon later inspection a hairline crack in the block that I hadn't noticed under the single lamp in the garage. I returned immediately, furious that I had lost everything in the world (my £60) and demanded my money back - which I got - as well as picking up a few tricks of the trade: 'Buyers Beware' and the 'Moonlight Motor' trick, both very common in those days.

Determined not to be outdone I bought a Hudson Terraplane from a man in Barking, but still had no work, so set about to find some. I began distributing pamphlets door-to-door advertising a car hire

Wt. 21115/DT733. 10,000 Pads. 9/46. B.B.LTD. 51-7213.

Form S. 1599

DUPLICATE—To be sent to Officer or Rating.

RELEASE

WAR GRATUITY & POST WAR CREDIT of WAGES
to be deposited in the POST OFFICE SAVINGS BANK

P.O.S.B. ACCOUNT PARTICULARS

H.M.S. "HORNBILL"

No. 2249

SURNAME (in block letters)	MR. MRS. MISS PETCHEY
Full Christian Names	Jack
Rank or Rating and Official No.	LAF(L) FX 523754
Permanent Address (give full postal address) ..	48 Goldsmith Avenue, Manor House London E.12
Date when amount is due to be deposited in the Savings Bank	31 Oct. 1946.

	Service		Unpaid Time	Not reckonable Service	Assessable Rank or Rating	Rate	Amount Payable		
	From	To	Days	Months		per month	£	s.	d.
War Gratuity	9-3-43	15-8-46 Terminal Est		36	LAF(L)	12/-	21	12	-
Post War Credit of Wages in respect of Service as a Rating after 31-12-41.	9-3-43	30-6-46 Terminal Est	Days 1054	— —		per day 6ᵈ	26	8	6.

		£			
Total amount of War Gratuity and Post War Credit	£	48	-	6.
Less deduction in respect of outstanding charges on pay account, etc.	£			
Amount for deposit	£	48	-	6.

Date of dispersal to leave 22-11-46

Date of termination of Foreign Service Leave

Date of release 17-1-47

Signature and rank of Certifying Officer

Date 25 November 1946

My War Gratuity - added to my meagre savings -
all spent on a car!

service, a relatively new concept in those days. My father disapproved greatly of this tactic and had choice words to say on the subject, but I wasn't complaining as the pamphlets did their job and the business started to flood in.

With few responsibilities, being a single man (but with high HP repayments) I was able to throw myself headlong into my new venture. I went down to the Royal Docks to meet any boat that came in, day or night, to tout for business. I charged 12s 6d from the dock to Kings Cross or Euston Station. This touting for business proved successful and when I later owned a fleet of white wedding cars I used a similar tactic and persuaded a local vicar to give me the names on the Wedding Banns, enabling me to approach the happy couples personally with the offer of a nice, brand new, Ford Consul for their Big Day. Pretty unconventional in that day and age, but it worked a treat! Business got better and better, and I worked harder and harder.

Christmas Day in 1948 was not a day you would want to break down. I did, however, finding myself stranded and unable to detect the fault. With a passenger in the car and without the required mechanical knowledge, I started to panic but was saved by a passer-by who had no problem finding the fault and sent me on my way. Unknown to me at the time, this man turned out to be Fred Milchard, a cousin of my good friend Ginger Barrow. Fred and I went on to be great mates and he helped me a lot during these early days of my car hire venture.

Trade was good and the money was coming in steadily - so much so that I was in a position to do something about our living arrangements. Mother was paying rent of £1.25 a week for 48 Goldsmith Avenue, so together we approached the landlady and agreed terms to purchase for £800 as a 'sitting tenant'. Immediately selling it for £1,200, vacant possession, before the contracts were even completed, it became my very first trade in the property business.

By the time the sale was complete I had negotiated to buy the lease on a property at 739 Romford Road, Manor Park - a small ground floor garage with living accommodation upstairs. We moved in immediately. Part of the £400 lease on the property also included a Minerva and Buick - two huge cars built around 1931, before the days of battery powered starter motors, with large starting handles which required jumping on vigorously to turn the engines over.

Now, with premises and two cars, we were in business. Bert Earl - a legal executive at E. Edwards Son and Noice, Solicitors in East Ham - did the conveyances. E. Edwards Son and Noice, from that point on, did the vast majority of my legal work over the years and I still use their services to this day.

It was at this point in my life that I met Diane Harrison (or Di as I always called her) - my future wife. I was at the Green Man Public House in

Diane Harrison - soon to become Diane Petchey

Happy days - Di & myself

Chingford with Ginger Barrow, who recounts the story:

"I remember we made many journeys to pubs and other places of entertainment, trying to persuade landlords and barmen to display literature and handing out business cards. It was on one such expedition that we visited the Royal Forest Hotel in Chingford and met Di and her friend Dolly (I never did know her surname.) I believe we agreed to meet in the Green Man in Leytonstone and I remember us tossing a coin to sort out who would chat up whom, I kept that coin for a long time afterwards!"

Although Ginger and Dolly went their separate ways Di and I became "an item" and courted for a while before getting married in 1949 at East Ham Registry Office, and took a one night honeymoon in a flat above our friends' off-license in the Fulham Road. The very next day I was back driving the taxi and conducting business from Romford Road.

We kept the car hire business open 24 hours a day, with me sleeping on a camp bed behind the counter, with the front door wide open. Customers would pass by, ring the bell, wake me up and I'd be off on another fare. Di was particularly supportive and would work on the telephone for many an hour.

One evening Di and I were driving down Goldsmith Avenue, and outside Number 48 stood my father, bags packed, and on the point of leaving. Not wishing to witness what we thought might have been an embarrassing moment, we simply drove on -

and that was the last time I ever saw him, standing there in the street.

Gradually I started adding more second hand cars to my fleet, employing drivers and proudly laid claim to being the first car hire service in East London that was equipped with two-way radios.

In 1949 I often drove Ronnie Orme, the MD of Icelandic Airlines, to and from airports to meet planes - mostly at about 4 o'clock in the morning. He took a liking to me and I told him how I had written to the New York office of an airline flying into London - and what poor response I had received. "Get up off your arse - and go and see them" he immediately told me! "I can't afford the flight" I replied. "If I flew you out for free, would you go?!!". "Yes, I would!"

My flight out was over the North Pole, and we landed on an expanse of wilderness to re-fuel at an old Nissen hut on a snow bound airfield where we got out for a good stretch - and to warm our hands over a coke fire in the hut - in the dark - it was such a frightening experience!

Then - to add insult to injury - having visited the New York office I was told that the matter was dealt with "locally", ie London - so I transferred my interest to Leadenhall Street in the City of London, where I was given tiny snippets of business - but, as they say, every little helped!

May 4th 1950 was a day to remember - Di gave birth to my first daughter Jacqueline (after whom the

My first Car Hire office in the Romford Road, Manor Park, E12

restaurant in Clube Praia da Oura - Jac's Brasserie - is now named). She was the apple of my eye, and I determined there and then that, now having extra responsibilities, my family would never look back. I would buy bigger and better houses, until we reached the top!

Life was not exactly without excitement, either. The East End of London was haunted by villains, and when they'd done a "job" - and were in the money - it became blatantly obvious as they would buy drinks all round in the local pubs, which told everyone they had just been "successful" - not to mention the plain clothed police that would hang around the pubs waiting for inside information! They also showed their hands by hiring chauffeur-driven cars to take them round the area, visiting various pubs along the way, showering the drinkers with free drinks - proper showmen they were.

On one occasion four of them hired me to take them pub-crawling, then up to Hyde Park, where they picked up a "lady of the night" who they took into the bushes, one by one, with the others waiting in the car with me. After all four had been with the "lady", they said "Your turn Jack". I was petrified at the thought so replied "Sorry, I've got no money". "Don't worry about that Jack, we'll pay". I had real difficulty in defending my "virginity" - but they eventually agreed to give me a good tip instead of paying for the lady's services! I know for certain that Di would have killed me if ever she thought I had availed myself of her services!

On another occasion three fellows - regular users of our Car Hire service - phoned up for a car to pick them up in Dagenham - and asked for their regular driver, Ken Crispen. Ken was out on another run, so I volunteered and picked my passengers up as directed. They instructed me to drive along the A13, then without warning, said "Turn left here Jack - quick, quick - over to that water tank over there". Instinctively I did as I was told - drove over a piece of waste land to an empty water tank, whereupon they jumped out, kicked over the tank and picked up various parcels that had been hidden there. They threw these parcels into the car and urged me to "Move, move, move!". My whole mind began racing in panic - what if the police had been watching and waiting! What if they saw what happened and surrounded the car! What if they thought I was part of the gang, instead of an innocent driver? What if? What if? I had visions of myself being clapped in jail, and in desperation, put my foot down and screamed off down the road. They delivered their parcels to a nearby shop, collected their ill gotten gains, and paid me off, much to my relief!

Funnily enough after that, each time they called to hire cars - we were, unfortunately, very busy, with no available cars at that moment! Not an experience I would have cared to repeat.

Goldsmith Avenue was also the haunt of 'Bookie's Runners' - people would give them money to put bets on horses for them - strictly illegal, but it

In and out of uniform!

went on all the time. We used to take it in turns to warn these Runners if a 'copper' passed by - until, of course, they got the measure of us, and warned us off.

Business continued steadily for the next 6 years, by which time my next daughter, Susan, had made her entry into the world in 1952. I made the decision to scrap my fleet of second hand cars - due to constant mechanical failures - and purchase a brand new fleet of Ford Consuls. It was around this time that I also sold my very first car. A customer had approached me to buy his car as he was in need of the money and having bought my new fleet and having scrapped all of the second hand cars, I had no use for it in a business sense, but did offer to put it on my forecourt for him. Within hours of being on the forecourt it sold, just like that, a proverbial hotcake so to speak, and with it came the birth of a new venture as I realised how easy it could be to sell cars, with none of the hard work entailed in the taxi trade!

Soon operating on a sale or return basis I was being asked to sell far more cars than I had the space to show them. Reluctant to turn away any business I took over the adjoining property, a paper storage warehouse and a coal order office with a stable behind, and before long I was displaying a vast range of second hand motor vehicles. I was on a roll.

During my first years of car trading I did come up against a few obstacles. On one such occasion a

Di Petchey - manning the phones at the Car Hire desk, behind which I would sleep to avoid losing any business.

Nice suit!

man bought a fibreglass-bodied sports car on hire purchase, only he failed to fulfil his obligations on the payments, so I simply went around to his house after dark and took the car back to the forecourt at Manor Park. Two mornings later I arrived at work to find that the man had pulled the very same stunt as I, and taken the car off the forecourt! The very same night I returned and recovered the vehicle yet again, this time putting it out the back with other cars parked in front of it. In a feat that has to be admired for sheer nerve, the man and his friends returned in the dead of night and simply lifted the car *over* the others and once again took it from the premises. I again returned to his house only to find that he had well and truly hidden it away this time, and I was unable to retrieve it. I made a point of returning to this man's house whenever I could, and subsequently found the car three weeks later, parked outside. This time, upon recovery of the vehicle and not to be outwitted, I made arrangements for it to be placed in a lock-up garage. At 9am the next morning I arrived to find the man waiting for me with a 'friend' in hand - a hatchet! Raging mad and waving the chopper around like a maniac, the man issued several threats in a bid to make me return the car, but I stood my ground - albeit scared for my life - and eventually he gave in and completed the payments, upon which he received his car in return. An episode which I now look back on in amusement, and often recount the tale.

This wasn't the only experience I had with non-payment; here an old friend Peter Wilkinson recalls another such situation.

"One Saturday night Jack asked if I would help him snatch back a car from a client who had not made his payments. After enlightening the police as to our intentions we made our way to a block of flats not far from the Dartford Tunnel where the car, a Ford Zephyr, was parked outside. Jack had given me a duplicate key and I started the car and not being familiar with it, put the headlights on full beam. While fiddling around the owner came running down the street, arms waving and screaming at the top of his lungs. With a screech of tyres I shot off back to the Romford Road showroom where Jack was waiting, knowing that the owner of the car had recently been released from prison, I asked Jack 'what for' to which he replied simply: 'GBH'.

In August 1957 Di gave birth to our son, John. Bert Earl, my solicitor and drinking buddy, remembers it well - or rather his wife Joan does:

"Jack knocked on our door at 5.30 in the morning to say that Di had gone into labour and to ask if Joan could sit with her while he went to fetch her mum and the midwife. Joan threw a dressing gown on and off she went. Upon his return at roughly 8am she left, only for her pyjama bottoms to fall down in full view of the early morning commuters while she crossed the road. She always said that it was the most embarrassing moment of her life!"

Bert had tried to discourage me from buying a brand new house in Upminster - but funnily enough, having visited us there, he moved into the very same street within a month! While we were both living so close, we asked him to look after our house on occasional weekends while we went away. Twice disasters befell poor Bert in doing this small favour ... once we had left a paraffin heater in the lounge, and the fuel ran out, emitting thick black oily smoke, which literally covered everything - including the canary! On another occasion - in the middle of a particularly vicious, freezing winter - Bert's wife visited one Sunday afternoon to find that the goldfish bowl had frozen solid. In her attempt to release the poor goldfish inside, she actually broke it in two in its frozen state! Imagine having to explain *that* to your children! We can laugh about it now, but at the time Bert & his wife were pretty upset.

By the end of the decade and the start of the 'Swinging Sixties' I came to the conclusion that I could sell many more cars if only I had more showroom space to do so. I bought a derelict piece of land on the Barking Road in East Ham and constructed a purpose built showroom with space for 50 cars together with 21 flats above, and installed a set of petrol pumps on the forecourt. I also introduced a fleet of self-drive cars and was the first dealer in London to have a fleet of chauffeur-driven white Ford Consul wedding cars, of which I

My fleet of white wedding Consuls

was immensely proud. To this day I still have a photo of those cars in my office, to remind me of my dreams and aspirations all those years ago.

Around this time, Di and I thought it would be beneficial for our son, John, to attend a boarding school in Norfolk. Naturally this required a uniform from a large store in Norwich. Of course, being a woman, Di disappeared off into the store, and started browsing. Bored, I sat in a chair in the Gardening Department, and waited for her to return. I made myself so comfortable that I fell asleep! At 6.10pm I was awoken by a Security Guard, telling me that the store had closed - and I was the only

**Opening the new Petchey Showroom in East Ham
My bow tie was soon to become a trademark.**

customer still inside! Di and John were nowhere in sight, either in or outside the shop, so I drove round and round the local vicinity in a vain attempt to find them. In a right old temper, I finally drove back to the store - to find them waiting outside - equally annoyed! A few terse words were spoken, but luckily we all ended up laughing about the incident, and John went happily off to school in his new uniform.

Steadily expanding all the time, I acquired a garage firm in the East India Dock Road with a workshop, and signed up for the agencies to sell Austin and Riley cars (the directors of which I later upset with some of my more 'radical' advertising ideas, particularly those with pump attendants on roller skates and bikini clad girls draped over my cars, which got me into hot water with the church as well) taking me into the Repair & New Car business for the first time. However, the business coup which pleased me the most was the take-over of Woods Motors at the Elephant & Castle. I paid £205,000 for it, then closed down the business and sold the premises for £351,000. I'd certainly have liked to have done a deal like that every year.

I had come a long way in those few years, I was running a successful Car Hire firm and trading in both automobiles and property, not bad for someone deemed 'not management material'.

Adver

th

rom

960's

MEET OUR

SMART

YOUNG

LADIES

SAYS JACK PETCHEY

KEY RINGS
PENCILS
BALLOONS
SWEETS
SERVICE
CIVILITY
AIR
ROAD MAPS!

FREE

THIS SATURDAY & SUNDAY

with every 4 gallons of Esso from

PETCHEYS

AD (near Bolyn), E.13 GRA 9531   557-565 BARKING ROAD, E.6

THERE'S JUST TIME!!

YOU CAN STILL GET YOUR
NEW AUSTIN FROM PETCHEYS
IN TIME TO GO VISITING
THIS CHRISTMAS!

YOUR **AUSTIN** DEALER

PETCHEYS

*Give a man a fish -
you feed him that night.*

***TEACH** a man to fish ...
and you feed him for
LIFE.*

Chapter Four

Winning Friends & Influencing People

~ Chapter Four ~

Winning Friends and Influencing People

During those first years of business I discovered Dale Carnegie – or did he discover me? I'm not sure! **How to Win Friends & Influence People** and **How to Stop Worrying & Start Living** are the books responsible for helping to develop, utilize and sharpen my business, management and marketing skills as well as playing a part in many other aspects of my life.

I had begun to take working very, very seriously indeed, with a burning ambition to reach the top. With this came depression – or more likely just plain worry – and I was treated by our family doctor, who suggested that I needed a holiday to relax – not something I do easily, even now. My expanding family (by now I had three children, Jacqueline, Susan & John) obviously benefited from the holidays, and I must admit that I enjoyed our times away, although never quite got into the habit of totally forgetting about my work life.

This happened several times and during one consultation with the doctor, he explained that people like me create their own vicious circle – they

*Family holiday at
Bigbury-on-Sea, South Devon.*

work too many hours – get depressed – go away for
a holiday – come back refreshed and happy – and
because they felt so refreshed, they return to the
long working hours that caused the problem in the
first place! And so the cycle starts again – nothing I
could do, either work less, or live with it.

I reflected long and hard on this and felt that I
didn't want to carry on like this for ever. One day I
noticed an advert claiming "How to start living and
stop worrying" – which was for a course
commencing at the Valentine Public House at Gants
Hill, Ilford – comparatively close to where I lived
and worked at the time.

Nothing ventured, nothing gained, I attended the introductory course and then signed up for a 13 week course, which consisted of one evening a week teaching the theories of Dale Carnegie, then practice the other six evenings – and was amazed that at the end of the thirteen weeks, I felt a lot better.

At the end of the course I was selected to help teach on the next 13 week course – which I happily did – and learned so much more by teaching than I had learned on the first course. I was also asked to help with marketing presentations as a past student and I did a memory test from a blackboard in front of potential students. This consisted of listing out twenty items – in numerical order – I was then blind-folded – and the lecturer listed out the items on the board which I had to memorise. Of course, there is an easy way to do this – but I won't tell you what it is – you'll have to attend the course yourself!

From here I went on to purchase books by Dale Carnegie, and found them to be more than helpful – and to this day practice many of the analytical theories that I found in the books. I encourage my staff – and friends – to practice one very simple and straightforward problem solving exercise – which is, of course, meant merely to clarify your thoughts – and many, many people have remarked on the fact that after having completed one of these exercises, they have found it helped to crystalise their thinking patterns, and have used the same method again and again. An old pal, David Webb – ex-Chelsea FC

On the piste!

defender – has even said that the number of books I give away on the subject – and the way I expound the theories, he thinks I am really Dale Carnegie himself – or at least getting commission on the sale of his books – which, unfortunately, I don't! Even now, I practice what I learned all those years ago, and often extol the virtues of the simple sayings in the books. In fact, I regularly send reminders of these "positive thinking" messages to people, including many of the youth clubs that participate in our Jack Petchey Foundation Achievement Awards – and they remark on how useful they find them.

Having enjoyed the Dale Carnegie course, I enrolled in the Ashridge Management College, and went to weekend and short management courses – several in fact, as I immensely appreciated both the course content, and meeting many senior people, with a vast amount of differing experience, from other companies and various trades. At that time I seemed to soak up information like a sponge and learned a great deal from these courses, and from the way these other people conducted their business lives – there's nothing like first hand knowledge to get the thought processes moving.

One group I particularly remember, were three people from the United Dairies – a very prominent dairy, which did doorstep deliveries in those days. They were preparing a marketing exercise for 2 years ahead – I, myself, was planning for the next week. It was from these 3 people that I was introduced to the benefits of forward planning and not running "by the seat of your pants".

At one of these courses there was an instance when the lecturer would project a face on a screen and ask "Who sees the face of an old lady?". Some 50% put their hands up. "OK, who sees the face of a young man?" – and the other 50% of hands shot up. The tutor then outlined the face of an old lady – and then outlined the face of a young man – and again it was obvious it was a young man. What it actually taught us was that people see or read the same "picture" or "message" differently – it's the way they look at it – or perceive things. Very similarly, people with differing attitudes – ie pessimists would look at a glass of water and see it half empty – whereas optimists would look at the same glass and see it as being half full – simply a difference in attitude.

Lateral thinking was also on the agenda – and it really does help, many a problem has been solved by this method.

The knowledge I gained on these courses has been immense and only recently I looked back on some of the coursework and realised that I still use some of the very same exercises some 50-odd years later! My first "Business Plan" – when I decided to break into the property investment market, was simply jotted down on a piece of paper on a spiral top notepad – and I have kept this as a reminder all

Taking my educational holiday VERY seriously!

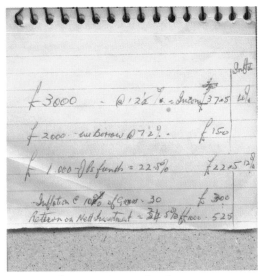

My very first "Business Plan"

these years, and often remind myself that sometimes the simplest of calculations really do work!

Wanting to also brush up my knowledge of financial matters, I enrolled on a Saturday morning course at the London School of Economics which was located close to the Embankment, south of the Strand. As it turned out, the lecturers – and the majority of the students – were very "left wing" – so rather than leave my car – a Rolls Royce – parked outside, I would have to park it several blocks away and walk to all the lectures. Then after the lectures had finished, I had to be extremely careful not to be seen driving the car away! Now I would probably say "what the hell", but then it seemed the most discreet way of doing things.

In the late 1960's Di surprised me with the news

that our family was about to expand yet again and in 1968 Amanda Jane was born, a much loved sister for Jackie, Susan and John.

Having dealt in cars for some years, I sold one of the showrooms and realised that this was far more profitable than selling dozens of cars and broke into the "property game" – sometimes with joint partners – sometimes on my own. One of these partners was Leslie Stolkin and together we purchased the Guilford Hotel in Sandwich Bay, Kent – which was not the best of projects – although my family became proud owners of an awful lot of crockery and cutlery that we disposed of when we refurbished! The location was aesthetically good – but I recall that a bitterly cold easterly wind absolutely howled there – or at least it did whenever I visited!

Our property purchases were quite diverse – from car showrooms to petrol stations to offices – to shops - to a large trading estate in Great Yarmouth – which caused an enormous amount of administrative work – to factories and blocks of flats. One of these apartment buildings was Roding Lodge, which consisted of Police flats – which were refurbished and a former Motor Trader friend, Bill Westlake, sold from the show flat at weekends.

However, things were definitely not all plain sailing. We had bought and sold property now for some 20 years, enjoying a steady, if not healthy, cash flow, but as it turned out 1974 was not to be a good year! The UK bank rate went up to a whopping

15%. Values of properties crashed, but the loan rate stayed the same. The bank foreclosed on us and demanded that we sold two of my properties to pay off the loan.

I sat for three nights, head in hands – did and re-did my sums, and realised, to my dismay, that although our assets were worth more than our debts, we did not have the money, nor income, to support the cash flow requirements! If we quickly sold any assets, we would not get a real price, and would go broke – skint! Not a pleasant thought! On top of this, I had invested in a holiday complex in Portugal – which I will tell you about in another chapter – and was desperate not to lose this as well.

In great anxiety I phoned my solicitor, Brian Edwards, who came to see me at 7 o'clock in the evening – as I was due to sign over one of our properties in Rayleigh the very next morning. We sat and mulled things over, and he gave me some advice, which I took, I'm glad to say.

With absolutely nothing to lose, the following morning, in great trepidation, I telephoned the bank to tell them that we had decided that we were NOT going to sign over the Rayleigh property. "You ARE" replied the Bank Manager. "I'm NOT" I retorted. "You ARE" he bit back. "I'm NOT " I replied, wishing that I was feeling as confident as I sounded! After a rather protracted and heated debate, we finally settled on another repayment plan which would leave us with SOME money – not a lot

– but not broke.

The moral of this sad tale is "Don't borrow more than you can afford to lose – as they say now – interest rates can go UP as well as DOWN". Also – always keep up to date accounts, including cash flows. We now have monthly cash flows, for all my businesses, and they are watched carefully to make sure that we never, ever have that sort of cash flow problem again. Once bitten, twice shy, as they say.

By this time our offices were situated above a car showroom in Romford Road, Forest Gate – and I had been advised that the way forward was to invest in the latest office equipment. Our accountant, Joe Moore, bought a second hand franking machine, which would save our book-keeper a lot of time in sticking stamps onto envelopes – and when he asked me what advert I wanted put on the envelope – I apparently replied "Pay Up!" – most of the correspondence being sent out being invoices and statements – not to mention a few Final Demands to many of our tenants! We further invested in a comptometer – a huge calculating machine – which was so noisy that it was relegated to a room of its own – together with its operator, Anne Laing, a tall girl with a particularly dry sense of humour, who stayed with the company for some 27 years before, sadly, passing away from cancer.

Our offices moved, yet again, to one of the factory units that I owned – Whitefields Factory – in Plaistow – three separate offices and shared facilities. In those days – before word processing machines – all typing had to be done on a clanking manual typewriter, with a black and red ribbon – and as I was careful with money, I insisted that the ribbon be used until the red had turned pink, and the black was pale grey. When we modernised our office and bought an electric typewriter my new secretary, Barbara – who incidentally is still with me after almost 34 years – was most amused when I asked her to re-use the ribbon – something that you just could not do, as it was made out of plasticised paper – it came as quite a shock to me that ribbons were ordered by the half-dozen, each month, rather than singly per year! She, of course, had no idea of my previous brush with bankruptcy – and I, of course, had little experience with the world of expensive electrical office equipment with constantly replaceable consumables!

It was my accountant, Joe, and secretary, Barbara, who extolled the virtues of using a computer for routine tasks – Barbara having worked for IBM for several years before coming to work for me. We scoured the market and found a company with a computer capable of handling the business – called a Q1 – on which Joe and Barbara spent many hours setting up accounting, word processing and credit control systems. My part-timer book-keeper, Jean, I remember, was petrified that this computer – which now languishes in a museum, no less – would make her redundant and flatly refused to give up her books and laboriously carried on doing everything in long-hand, shunning the dreaded Q1 in the corner! We did, eventually, find her other accounting duties – but to the day she left – also after 27 years service - she was still eyeing our, by then, large computer system with complete distrust!

Joe Moore – a straightforward Irishman – was not only my accountant, but our credit controller and bailiff too. If any of our tenants would, or could, not pay, it was he who knocked on their doors, demanding the rent – and more than often got it! He was a stickler for procedures and licked the office staff into shape – a good disciplinarian, but very fair. A thoroughly good, God-fearing man, whose wife sadly suffered from kidney failure; he not only worked unstintingly for us, but regularly hooked her up onto the dialysis machine too – a great worry for him. When she died, simply because her veins collapsed and she could not take any more dialysis, Joe threw himself into fund-raising for HARP, which was a charity formed for kidney patients at the London Hospital. After the death of his wife, Joe never stopped helping charities – one of life's good, honest men. Sadly Joe passed away in 2013 after a long battle with illness. Along with his funeral in Ireland, a memorial service was held in Portugal, attended by many of the friends and colleagues that Joe had known over the years - I think that is testament to what a well respected and popular man he was. I feel very lucky to have known him in both a professional and personal capacity and he remained a good friend right up until he sadly passed. Before he died he kindly shared some of his memories for this book and here recollects when he first joined the company.

"I well remember my initial meeting to discuss employment with Jack. Having gone over my CV and Jack questioning me at great length, the subject of tax was raised. I remarked that as an Irishman with 600 years of rebel blood in my veins, I had a natural antipathy to paying tax, particularly to an English government. Jack gave me the coldest of looks and I thought I'd blown it there and then. On the way home I thought to myself, 'Well Joe, just keep trying to get a job somewhere else'. However when I got home I received a telegram asking for date on which I'd like to start, so I must have said something right!"

Joe would regularly visit the St. Nicholas Trading Estate in Great Yarmouth – collecting rents – and taking stick from some of the more recalcitrant tenants – most of whom had varied excuses for not paying, from leaking roofs to non-paying customers of their own, not to mention hastily compiled sob stories. However, this estate was a good source of income for several years, and I imagine that the tenants heaved sighs of relief when they saw the back of Joe after his regular three monthly rent-collection visits.

We carried on investing in properties – some

rather more lucrative than others – and in 1981 moved offices yet again – out of necessity as we could no longer squeeze the necessary extra staff into our present premises. This time we moved into - what we thought then – plush, large offices above a former furniture showroom in the Barking Road, Plaistow, the showroom having burned down, which we redeveloped into a frozen food supermarket. Our office space had more than trebled, and from then on it seemed that we never looked back. With extra staff came extra computers, and our trusty Q1 was relegated to the back of a cupboard. A far more modern, networked system took its place – along with some 8 or 9 new staff – and Joe had his work cut out for him then! Very soon a Computer Manager also became a 'must', not to mention an Office Junior and a Tea Lady to cater for the growing staff numbers!

Of course, not all our property investments were wise ones – I remember, quite vividly, the problems we had when we bought the ex Laporte Chemicals site in Ilford. This had very good potential – but unfortunately had serious contamination issues, the implications of which resulted in far more work than envisaged – and more Government red tape that I ever wish to get involved with ever again! A big mistake, and one that I was very glad to sell on. But, of course, more experiences under my belt.

Our acquisitions were building into a very healthy portfolio – and very soon we had a resident

Property Manager, taking over the property details from Joe, ably assisted by Henry Jones, a hard-working, well trusted surveyor who had worked in a consultant capacity for us from the outset of our property trading activities, having been introduced by Leslie Stolkin, my first joint venture partner.

I then teamed up with Victor Gray, a former business acquaintance who already had property dealings, and together we purchased the Purfleet Industrial Park – which was destined to become a winner due to its proximity to a major road, the A13, which ran from Southend to London - an ideal position. However, unfortunately, this acquisition proved to be a nightmare – Vic, unlike me, was not a man for paperwork, and our management meetings were fraught with disaster – and in the end we agreed to differ, and parted company. The estate was finally sold, but too soon for the long anticipated A13 redevelopment to have any effect, and it turned out to be not quite the money-spinner I had imagined – and it had soured a once excellent relationship. Still – as they say – you can't win 'em all!

Swift on the heels of the Purfleet Industrial Park, I was introduced to a half-finished industrial park, the Lorimar Trading Estate, only about a mile away. Within a year all the units had been completed – and this time we realised the profit potential, and now that the A13 has finally been completed, you can actually see the estate from the road – a wonderfully sited estate, with good links to the M25, Tilbury and Docklands. Maybe we should have hung on to it, I will never know – but it doesn't pay to look back on "what ifs" – I prefer to look to the future.

By this stage, all our office procedures were computerised, with mail shots, invoices and statements being sent out as if by magic on the correct due dates! The number of staff had almost quadrupled! Communication was largely by telex – quite revolutionary in those days – you could type at a large console, dial up the number of a corresponding console in another office or country even – and the message was typed out on that other console – along with a long white tape, punched with holes, which Barbara could even translate through "reading" the pattern of holes. Then it would have been difficult to believe that within 10 years we would be using instantaneous faxes and then emails – concepts that were far beyond the realms of our imaginations. To us, the telex machine was very hi-tech – and, of course, considerably cheaper than using the telephone, plus you had the added bonus of a printed copy of your communication, even though you had to tear the sheet from the huge roll of paper, so none of the copies were ever the same size.

I thought that things could never get better, but in time, of course, this wonderful mechanised office equipment was declared to be archaic – and even more electrical apparatus arrived – until we had more and more of the latest, up to date equipment on the market – and had to provide a room especially for it!

By 1988 even this large suite of offices became insufficient, and as we took on more and more staff, it became necessary to buy two more offices – one named very aptly "Carnegie House" after my – unbeknown to him – mentor, Dale Carnegie. The other office – Exchange House, in Ilford – is the one that we operate from now – although whether this will be our last – who knows – only time will tell!

Yesterday is history ...

Tomorrow is a mystery ...

Today is a gift ...

*That is why it is
the "present".*

Chapter Five

A Place in the Sun

~ *Chapter Five* ~

A Place in the Sun

"Location, Location, Location" is a phrase that has become something of a cliché over the years but in the 1970s it certainly rang true for me as far as Portugal was concerned.

In the latter part of the 1960s I saw great potential in Portugal and the Algarve in particular, where the tax laws were less draconian than our own. It was then that I met for the first time two men who were to play a great part in the upcoming events, Graham Adams and Malcolm Fraser, who had met each other in the Arctic of all places, where amongst other things, they had been involved in a mining exploration company, which, by their own admission, had made and lost them a fortune.

I had been to Portugal on a number of occasions and was frustrated at not being able to start a project with the people I was working with. On my way home from one of my visits, my flight out of Faro airport was delayed and I met a woman by the name of Tina da Sousa who had an estate agency and was in partnership with Knight Frank & Rutley, who recommended that I should contact Graham and Malcolm about working together to start a project in the Algarve.

Graham, Malcolm & I spoke briefly on the phone and agreed to meet in my car showroom, which they expected to be a "four pump garage" and not the large showroom with a Rolls Royce parked out front. I agreed to a partnership - 50% for us and 50% for Malcolm and Graham - to build tourist accommodation in the Algarve. They had started to build eight villas and I said that we would finish them, and they should look for a bigger project.

Some months later we were informed that Senor Viera, who owned most of the land at Praia da Oura (as well as being Mayor of Albufeira) was interested in selling some of it. Convinced that it was a winner, Graham phoned me from Portugal, eager to start our new venture. 'When do you need me there?' I asked. 'Yesterday' was Graham's reply. The very next day saw us standing on the cliff overlooking the Atlantic Ocean gazing at the rippling waves in the bright sunshine and watching the tiny fishing boats bobbing up and down on the horizon. I knew immediately that it was a perfect place for a holiday resort and thought to myself 'One day thousands of tourists will wake up to this view'. We discussed the possibilities, Graham said we could do various parts of this large project and after some deliberation I said 'let's do the lot' - which turned out to be over 600 apartments.

With the help of Manuel Figuero, a 'larger than life' lawyer (who later died as he had lived, in a high speed car accident) we worked solidly for four

'One day thousands of tourists will wake up to this view.'

days to negotiate, draft and sign the contracts.
Standing on the cliff at the Golden Beach, with
contracts in hand, I couldn't help but have some
reservations. 'I'm not sure if it would be worse now
if you or I fell over the edge' I told Graham, to which
his reply was 'If you're going to jump - sign this
first!' So from first sight to contracting what was to
be Clube Praia da Oura took only four days!

At the time we were told by more than one
person that we were crazy to pay such a high price
for the land. Years later we were told how *lucky* we
were.

With the paperwork done, now came the
planning. At the time of purchase we had outline
planning in the form of defining density, how much
construction could be built, but no actual design
work done. We liked the work of Architect Ramos
Chaves, but the mayor wanted us to use the town
Architect, Norberto Correia. This was the first of

many problems we were to encounter. Outraged at being told who to use, we promptly refused, but later realised that this could seriously hinder our efforts, so eventually came to a compromise and agreed to use architects Ferreira Da Silva and Ramires Fernandes. Da Silva was resident architect for Vale da Lobo, a thriving holiday complex along the coast, and Fernandes was an up-and-coming young architect. Together they drew up the outline for a building of stepped pyramid design. It was pretty wonderful and everything we could have asked for, but with one obvious flaw; it encroached on land that we didn't own. Not wanting to change our ambitious plans we sought to discover the owner of the coveted piece of land, who turned out to be a very wealthy Dutch recluse by the name of Dr. Adrian Van Hall.

Van Hall took great pleasure in being rude and very difficult. Graham was dealing with the negotiations and will freely admit that this was a game of cat and mouse with himself firmly playing the part of distressed mouse. Now Graham, no pushover himself by any stretch of the imagination, eventually grew tired of Van Hall's rudeness and belligerence and while standing on the contested piece of land, lost his temper and told Van Hall to 'keep your land and stick it up your.....'. At this Van Hall broke into fits of laughter and from that day on he and Graham became firm friends until his death some years later.

Van Hall signed the provisional promissory contract but would not sign the escritura (legal deed of ownership) due to his love of playing the cat and mouse game. I was concerned and told Graham and Malcolm we had to do *something*. Enter at this point the infamous lawyer Dr. Jorge Abreu who was Manuel Figuero's partner. Throughout the history of Clube Praia da Oura, Jorge would assist us greatly with some of the more difficult problems we encountered.

With Van Hall, Jorge Abreu was asked by us to get him to the notary office to sign the escritura as we had the project designed and were ready to start (partially on the land Van Hall had to sign over). Jorge and Van Hall fortunately had two things in common - they both talked a lot and both drank a great deal. Jorge decided that the latter would be his strategy to lure him there. Dr. Batalha, the notary, was kept waiting for some time but eventually in staggered Jorge and Van Hall, to everyone's great relief, until it came to the actual signing that is. When Van Hall asked for the cheque Jorge decided that it was time for the cat to become the mouse and promptly took the cheque, put it in his mouth and began to chew. Fortunately Van Hall found this incredibly funny and after retrieving it from Jorge's mouth, Graham smoothed out the cheque and handed it to the Dutchman, who signed over the land - at long last.

We also decided at this point to buy the land behind what would become Blocks A and B, to allow for an entrance from the north as well as enabling us to build more apartments. As often happens in Portugal, land boundaries and land owners are obscure, and so it was with *this* particular piece of land. Eventually we discovered the owner, a Senor Palinha, who spent six months of the year working on fishing boats in Mozambique. Once back in Portugal Graham met with him and attempted to negotiate a deal but he asked such a high price that Graham put his foot down and declined. Off Palinha went back to the fishing boats in Mozambique. However, later we decided that we really wanted this piece of land for our north entrance and reluctantly agreed to the price. Upon meeting with Palinha he refused his original price and said the price was now *double*. Initially we were shocked and flatly refused but again decided that we wanted the land badly enough to offer more money (but not double). He flew into a rage, saying that we were robbing him etc, etc. We now stuck to our guns and said very firmly that this was our final offer. He made to leave, then turned around with a smile and finally agreed with 'OK you have a deal'.

So much for the foreigners outwitting the local simple people! This was constantly our experience; the local people were maybe not sophisticated, but were certainly shrewd negotiators.

We were in for yet another surprise when we went to the notary to sign the escritura. Senor

Palinha was one of *ten* brothers and sisters who owned the land. Two of them signed while the others - who could neither read nor write - put their fingerprints on the contract, but before they had all done this they demanded to see the money. We showed them the cheque but were told this was unacceptable! We offered to have the cheque certified but were told that this too was unacceptable - they would only take cash.

So off we went to the bank, which luckily had enough cash available, and took it back to the family, where it was put on the table in front of them. As the very last fingerprint was placed on the contract all hell broke loose as the money was devoured by the surge of eager brothers and sisters - if that money got divided equally then I'm a monkey's uncle!

Quite obviously a project of this size required a helpful bank and a large reputable construction company. For the bank we chose B.E.S.C.L. We arranged a meeting with the Vice President, Dr. Amaral, who kept us waiting until I finally decided this was taking it too far and told the secretary that 'we could not wait any longer, after all we had only come to borrow money from them!' Just as we were leaving the Vice President arrived and apologised, clearly surprised that we were willing to walk away and take our business elsewhere.

The bank eventually gave us the loan facility after sending someone to value the land (and outline planning) which they valued at four times what we had paid for it!!! We continued to have a good relationship with them until the Portuguese Revolution in 1974.

For the construction company, we chose Mitchell Construction (Portugal) - a subsidiary of Mitchell Construction (UK) who in turn were a subsidiary of the Kinere Moody group, probably the No.1 UK construction company at the time. We decided to work with them for all the associated benefits of working with a big company, not to mention their financial reliability. After nearly six months of negotiation we agreed to sign contacts, however on the very same day that we chose to sign, the parent company KMG went bankrupt! So much for working with a large financially reliable company!

After much discussion we decided that we didn't want to spend another six months negotiating with another company. So after investigations, Mitchell Construction (Portugal) which was said by the receivers, Coopers & Lybrand, to be profitable, and as the existing Managing Director was prepared to financially participate, we negotiated with the receivers to purchase all of the shares of Mitchell Construction (Portugal). Later we were to discover that the management accounts we were given had not been reconciled to what was called the fiscal accounts in Portugal, and most of the work in hand was, in fact, losing money. We could have sued

Coopers & Lybrand but that would have only lined the lawyers' pockets for a few years so we decided to cut our losses and move on. Mr. Cook, the Managing Director, resigned and Engineer Vidal became the MD and was the most efficient, organised person we encountered in Portugal - most unusual at the time!

The process of getting CPO designed and built was a long and arduous one. Graham ran the project meetings, which at the time took up to 10 hours and we also had the help of a British architect, John Goldsmith, Project Manager, Derek Rochford and a firm of quantity surveyors, George & Peter Venn. On reflection I am not sure whether this British professional help was of any benefit or not, as they were confronted with the same practices and attitudes that we ourselves had found so difficult. For instance John Goldsmith pointed out that it was strange to have an architectural design so far advanced with no detailed design existing for surface water draining - which was noted - but nothing changed.

In 1973 Malcolm was only spending part of his time in the Algarve and finally decided he wanted to live full time in London, so Graham and I bought his 25% share.

Before the construction started we came to the conclusion that the best market to aim at was the Portuguese themselves, as opposed to most other developers who were concentrating on foreign markets. We decided to sell to Portuguese Nationals

"Before"

with an 8% per annum guaranteed return for a lease back scheme. This was for a lease with the buyer being allowed to use the apartment for six weeks each year, plus a likely 15% per annum increase in value, i.e. approx 23% per annum. This was a very attractive package to Portuguese buyers, and also meant that we received an immediate return by not having to wait for foreign money. This was so successful we were selling before the building had begun. In fact the cash flow was so good the bank complained that we were not using our loan facility! So there we were, the best site on the Algarve and selling apartments like hot cakes without laying a single brick, what could possibly go wrong?

To cut an incredibly long story short - on 25th April 1974 a group of middle ranking officers from the Portuguese military calling themselves the Armed Forces Movement, overthrew the Caetano (ex Salazar) regime, which had ruled Portugal in an authoritarian manner for some 48 years, in a bloodless coup.

At first the situation at CPO reflected the rest of the country - nothing really happened - then the attitude towards Graham and myself from the local staff went from bad to worse - Graham was threatened constantly. During the height of the uprising a communist Prime Minister had been installed by the military (not elected) and the country was in a state of complete anarchy, even the soldiers stopped shaving and smoked on duty.

One of our first employees was Antonio Caetano, our Book-keeper/Accountant. He asked for an assistant and we took on a young lady, Ana Maria Rosa who was inexperienced but quickly established herself as someone who could get things done. We relied on her more and more as time went by and gradually Graham took Ana Maria on as his assistant, and over the years she rose in status within the company, before leaving us in 1980 to become a partner in a group of property companies. I'm happy to say that she returned to us again in 1997 as

"After" - quite a transformation

General Manager! After the Revolution, however, Ana Maria was "persuaded", along with the Workers Committees of both Mitchell Construction and CPO workers, to sign a form denouncing Graham and I to the Ministry of Labour, stating that we were doing things illegally (mainly taking money out of the country, which we were not). Ana Maria has later admitted that she only did it because she was frightened not to - and because Engineer Vidal, the Managing Director of Mitchell, had already done so! The only employees who did *not* sign the document were Graham's secretary, Sue Bland, and Carlos Vidal's secretary, and two or three junior employees.

Enter again our eccentric lawyer, Jorge Abreu, who went with Graham to meet the Minister of Labour. Once again - without us quite understanding how - Jorge managed to talk us out of the problem and he and Graham were escorted to the door of the Ministry of Labour by the Minister who was laughing, much to the consternation of the Workers Committee, who were sitting outside in the corridor.

In 1974 a law was passed that made it illegal to make workers redundant or put companies into liquidation, so as the number of foreign tourists reduced and our sales suffered we all felt the pinch financially, which could not be rectified by laying off staff. In fact at one stage we had purchased large amounts of furniture for the apartments but not being able to pay wages meant that some of the staff walked away with our furniture as payment.

Obviously a time came when we had to stop building. Blocks A and B were finished but there was still much to do on blocks C and D. This became a major problem as we were stuck with several hundred workers who we could not pay or make redundant due to the new law.

During this highly sensitive period of unrest, Graham and I were flying up to Lisbon almost on a daily basis in attempts to resolve some of our mounting problems. One Friday evening I was returning to England from Faro Airport, when I was asked by a desk clerk if I had any Escudos and I declared the equivalent of £100 which I understood to be the limit allowed. Army soldiers were called in and I was arrested for trying to take out more money than I was allowed. I pleaded my innocence showing them a sign on the wall stating the allowance, to which they replied 'that's only a sign, not the law!' Conveniently (for them) the law had been changed that same day reducing the export allowance to £50. I was eventually led off to Faro Court by armed soldiers at the end of more than one machine gun. At 1 o'clock in the morning the court convened - there was no electricity and the court was lit with candles - as I stood in the dock I saw my passport on the table and got a terrible urge to snatch it and run, however this was suppressed by an image in my head of the soldiers mowing me down in a hail of bullets as I made my daring escape!

I was released on bail with the stipulation that I had to return to Portugal in a month. I now found myself in a 'Catch 22' situation. If I returned and was convicted, I faced a minimum sentence of five years in prison, while on the other hand if I failed to return, all my assets in Clube Praia da Oura would be seized and I would be financially ruined. So I decided to return and answer the charges, thinking that the prison sentence was the lesser of two evils, at least this way I could hang on to CPO.

The case was adjourned on almost a monthly basis for the next two years when eventually the attitude and ambience towards foreigners changed and the case was eventually dismissed, another court case under my belt that luckily I walked away from.

I decided it would be a good idea to learn Portuguese - it seemed somewhat churlish to expect everyone at Clube Praia da Oura to speak English while I had not even the most basic knowledge of their language. I was advised to use the Linguaphone method and I duly set about listening to all the tapes. Languages not exactly being my forté, I was unsuccessful, so I decided to enrol in a college - only to find the other students not only speaking Portuguese fluently, but discussing - in Portuguese - the history and culture of the country! I am ashamed to admit that I gave up - and to this day only have a very rudimentary grasp of the language - luckily for me most of the staff at the resorts speak perfect English!

The revolution caused not only problems for myself but also put Graham in danger as he was threatened in various ways. He recounts just how serious it got:

"The CPO workers committee was gradually becoming more militant as the revolution progressed. The head of the committee was a man by the name of Palmer, who we believe was being controlled by the Communist Party. As the militants in Portugal, and specifically CPO, got their power they called a workers meeting. As well as the workers in attendance there were also people from the unions, Ministry of Labour and the Military - clearly this was no ordinary meeting. The committee presented charges against Sergio da Costa - General Manager of CPO and responsible only to me. I was there as an owner of the company and listened to the charges (which had no substance whatsoever) as

well as Sergio's rebuttal and said there was no case against him. At this stage a union/communist man stood up and began a tirade of abuse against Sergio and CPO, saying that this was not against myself - which was total rubbish as it was clearly I who was the real target. At the height of his tirade he shouted at workers 'Do you need money to live?' to which came a resounding 'Yes'. He followed with 'Therefore you need permanent work?' to which he received another cry of 'Yes'. This was followed by 'Do you want the "Saniado" of Sergio da Costa?" again he received screams of 'Yes', I later found out that Saniado meant 'to cleanse' and was the militants' word for getting rid of people and allowing them to take over their business. This was illegal as they had no legal power.

I was shocked and for the first time realised that law had no meaning whatsoever in Portugal any more. The next day I asked Palmer (who had been wandering around CPO brandishing a gun) to meet me in the office. I asked how he now saw the business operating. He replied that there would be very little change. Just that now the workers committee would be party to all management decisions and would countersign all cheques - not my idea of very little change!

From there things just got worse and I heard unofficially that I was about to be arrested (just what for I had no idea) but owners and administrators of other companies had been arrested without charges and simply locked away. A few workers who had remained loyal to me advised me to leave the country and arranged an illegal crossing into Spain as my name would be at all the frontiers. I was highly concerned because I had heard that others had been arrested without charges and jailed. Jack and I had been to the British Embassy earlier and asked if they would help in the event of being arrested. They smiled and said they would bring us tea and biscuits ... but couldn't guarantee being able to help. The whole problem came to a head when I held a meeting in the middle of the night at my house, with the loyal workers (strangely including Leonete, the CPO Housekeeper, who was an official in the Albufeira Communist Party) who were on the Workers Committee and who

Clube Praia da Oura stands proud on the Golden Beach

Clube Praia da Oura ... completed

privately reported to me so I could advise them on how to run the Workers Committee. These meetings were to our benefit, as well as changes going on throughout Portugal. Everyone knew I was about to leave the country and asked me to stay as they thought all the companies would stop operating if I left. I said that if I had definite assurance that if I stayed I would not be arrested, I would stay. The lawyer from Mitchell's said that he would attempt to get that assurance, being a card playing friend of Admiral Rosa Coutinha, who was one of three people currently in control of Portugal. I waited for 24 hours for the assurance, which did eventually come and I stayed.

With the help of the loyal workers, CPO and Portugal as a whole, returned to relatively normal functioning, helped, of course, by Jorge Abreu, our lawyer and friend, who handled the ever changing complex legal process and oversaw the sacking of Palmer after he had threatened to 'castrate Sergio da Costa by hand'. (He had apparently killed people in the war in Angola). Over the next few years things gradually got back to normal, sales began to increase, D Block was completed, and work commenced on other blocks. But feeling a bit "burned out" I decided to leave.

Graham's decision to leave came as a bit of a blow, but also raised a business opportunity, so the decision was made to buy out all his interest and head off later into the dizzying world of timeshare.

*Nothing is more certain
to strip the disguise from
a passable bit of muddled
thinking, than an effort
to set down clearly on
a piece of paper.*

Chapter Six

The American Connection

~ *Chapter Six* ~

"The American Connection"

Timeshare – or Holiday Ownership as it is now widely called – was introduced to me in 1980, and I visited resorts in America several times to understand the concept before taking it over to Clube Praia da Oura. I hired a team of Americans, headed by the larger-than-life character, Hank Hankins, and Walter McGee, a quieter, but nonetheless, charismatic man from Vero Beach in Florida. The American team had a major impact, and soon their yankee accents could be heard all over the resort, extolling the virtues of the timeshare concept, the beautiful grounds, the nightly entertainment, and so on.

Timeshare took off in a big way – with holiday-makers soon realising the benefits of owning a week or more, every year, at the resort. They didn't always have to take their holidays there, they could swap their weeks for holidays in other resorts around the world, using one of the two large exchange companies, already set up for the American timeshare market.

It wasn't long before necessity forced me to move our offices into much larger premises, to cope with the tide of ever-increasing paperwork, and very soon our staff had doubled. Our Accountant, Joe and my Secretary, Barbara, had the onerous task of compiling a procedures manual to ensure that all the staff were "singing from the same song sheet", and volumes of forms were soon set up for the different aspects of this new business.

Dozens of new owners turned into hundreds and very soon, thousands. I don't think even I had contemplated such a success. With this success came prosperity to the Golden Beach area, as new bars, restaurants and shops opened up to cope with the needs of the hundreds of holiday-makers, and the tiny village soon became a thriving town. The Americans – as they do – soon renamed the steep hill up into the village "Cardiac Hill" – for obvious reasons - and the main street became "The Strip". To this day, the names have remained, with everyone affectionately remembering how these titles came about.

It occurred to me that only people actually taking their holidays in the Algarve were being introduced to Clube Praia da Oura, and so toyed with the idea of opening an "offsite" showroom in London. Ideal premises were found in Leicester Square, and so the first offsite timeshare sales showroom was born. People were invited to view a presentation of Clube Praia da Oura, and timeshare in general, and each one was rewarded with a gift on departure – two lucky people even won brand new cars.

However, all was not plain sailing, and very

Two of the four cars presented to lucky winners at our CPO offsite office in Leicester Square by Leslie Grantham & Vicky Michelle.

soon our novel marketing tactics were noticed by a major TV programme, who set about to make a two week "exposé" of the business. It was then that I realised how another company could make people's lives a real misery. A TV crew camped on the doorstep of not only my office, but my home, where they constantly rang the doorbell, shouted through the letter box, and harangued all our visitors. At one time I felt like a prisoner and had to virtually "escape" by taking a route through the adjoining snooker hall, and down their fire escape! I had learned that it was great fun for these people to take sentences out of concept, and turn your words around, so declined to make any statements.

Each morning, millions of TV viewers were subjected to views of me "cowering" in my office, and uninvited camera crews barging their way through our beautiful holiday complex, not to mention scenes in front of my house where they were shouting through my letterbox – into an empty house – and intimating that I would not answer the door! It became a virtual nightmare, and my only recourse was to take them to the British Broadcasting Standards Commission for invasion of privacy and mis-statement of facts. However, by this time, the damage had been done, and timeshare had become a dirty word, thanks to this one television company. I never did find out why they took it upon themselves to do this, but I did, in fact, have the last word when the BBSC not only agreed with all our complaints against them, but also made them publish a public apology. Justice, as it were, had been done – but was it too late?

It was about this time that I had the idea of a London Timeshare, so I asked Graham Adams if he would like to be involved. We found a beautiful Georgian property in Kensington, Allen House, which was made up of large period apartments, some of which were rented to long term tenants, and some of which were holiday lets. I realised the potential here for a London timeshare, and very soon these apartments were selling to the foreign nationals like hot cakes, they being very fond of London, and loving these apartments for their Georgian architecture, and closeness to all the appeal of London ... the shops, the theatres, the landmarks, and not least, Buckingham Palace, where they all hoped to glimpse someone from the Royal Family. Of course, many UK buyers bought timeshare weeks because of their strong exchange power, enabling these owners to spend holidays in other high quality apartments around the world.

However, two of the long term tenants took offence at the apartments being marketed in this way, and soon complained to the Borough of Kensington & Chelsea about the selling methods – and once again, another battle on my hands! Of course, this entailed a summons to court, a mountain of paperwork, solicitors and barristers, and many sleepless nights, I can tell you! But ... I'm

Allen House, Kensington

delighted to say … the case was thrown out of court at the eleventh hour, with the judge saying there was no case to answer – phew …. another battle won, although by this time my hair had turned a silvery white!

In an attempt to set the records straight, I agreed to make a television interview – not the best decision I have ever made. I thought this would be my turn to present my point of view, and asked for questions to be prepared in advance to enable me to choose my words carefully. Having spent some days mulling over the answers to the questions, the office was soon filled with TV crew, lights, cameras pointed at me at every angle conceivable, and microphones positioned above, behind and in front of me … and it began… Not being the most eloquent of speakers, and wanting to make sure that everything I said was correct, I frequently paused for breath. At one point the lights being so hot, the interviewer suggested that I wipe my brow on my handkerchief … a fatal mistake. When the interview went out on TV to a million viewers, the brow-wipe was transmitted not once, but three times, in an attempt to make it look as though I was under pressure, and my pauses for breath looked like I was hesitating, trying to find the correct answer. My words were taken right out of context and in my view the whole interview was a disaster. Still, I'm sure that by the next day, it had been watched and forgotten, although certainly not by me … my confidence had been severely shaken, I can tell you! Not an experience I would care to repeat.

With all this bad press under my belt, I was determined that nothing would hinder the success of Clube Praia da Oura. We had started to produce twice-yearly newsletters, The Golden Beach News, and I continued these with optimism for the future. Clube Praia da Oura continued to flourish, and more and more holiday-makers continued to spend their timeshare weeks there. More apartments were built, and more amenities added – a "first" to the Algarve, a bowling green set on the cliff top, overlooking the ocean – saunas, better entertainment, a children's club, and all the apartments were completely refurbished to keep up with the ever increasing demands of our owners. We determined never to stand still, it being our intention that the Clube would remain the best in the Algarve for ever.

In time the Americans left the Algarve, probably to the dismay of the local bars and restaurants. We all missed their good humour and camaraderie, but respected their need to move on. Their places were filled with English and Portuguese sales teams who are still there to this day. I made a bad error of judgement at this point and entered into a joint venture with Walter McGee, purchasing a Spanish resort. Walter then relieved me of a very considerable sum of money by transferring funds to a French bank account, and "did the off", as they say. To this day I have been unsuccessful – together with the US Revenue Service, and his wife, in tracking him down! Still, it's all water under the bridge – but that's not to say that I wouldn't like to get my hands on him!

Back to the subject matter – timeshare. Business boomed and grew to include some 18,000 happy timeshare owners – and a staff of 30 in the Ilford office which provided management services – a far cry from the days when it all began – with just our initial accountant, Joe Moore, secretary, Barbara Staines and two part-time book-keepers, one of which, Anne Laing, who had been with us since our days at Westbury Court in Forest Gate, sadly died of cancer, and the other, Jean Mason, who retired after 27 years with the company. My secretary – for her sins – is still with me!

Our next venture was in Florida – and again it was a case of "Location, Location, Location" – only this time maybe the wrong place and the wrong time.

In 1988 Hank Hankins approached me to get involved in buying a golf course development in Florida that had gone bankrupt and was in the hands of an American Government Agency, the Federal Asset Disposition Association (FADA).

The golf course was beautiful and had held a PGA senior golf tournament, and was classified as a championship course. The real estate around the course consisted of several hundred lots with a few houses already built and 110 completed apartments that had been sitting empty for a few years.

Hank said that the legal issues were now sorted out and it could be bought "for a song".

I didn't have the time to spend on the idea, including the need to go to America, so I asked Graham Adams if he was interested in getting involved.

Due to Hank's previous successes at selling and the quality of the development, we bought the project and proceeded to put the 110 apartments back into good condition, and then went ahead with a strong marketing programme.

The good news was that Sam Sneed had a house there in the winter and agreed to be the Pro Emeritas.

The bad news was that the development was located between Vero Beach – a high class beach front town – and Fort Pierce, a town with lesser prestige with a less than desirable community – unfortunately we were closer to Fort Pierce. Graham and I believed Hank, who said that this would not be a problem.

Added to this, 1988 was the beginning of a property market collapse. Hence "wrong place, wrong time".

We tried extremely hard to overcome the problems, but eventually realised that we needed to sell the whole project, and cut our losses and move on. We sold the golf course to the members, held an absolute auction on the lots and finally sold the whole of the balance to another developer.

The sad part was the painful arthritis in my back did not even allow me to enjoy such a beautiful golf course!

It was a good lesson in attempting to do business in an area you don't know instead of your home turf. We also experienced at first hand, the American legal society. Our budget for legal expenses was woefully low! An example of this was someone who we should have sued (which is not our style) – sued us for $75,000 – the lawyer said we should settle for $25,000 even though we were not guilty as it would cost more than that for his fees to prove it! Someone else sued us for $1M but said he would settle for $10,000.

It was my first and last attempt at doing business in the USA. However, I'm pleased to say that it didn't put me off the country completely, as I fell in love with a particular area of Florida, where I spend my holidays - a perfect spot for relaxation, where you can jump out of bed, straight onto the jetty, fish before breakfast, and take a boat out into the ocean within 15 minutes. Needless to say, my now rapidly expanding, extended family, have also taken a liking to the same spot and often join me there. Our small piece of heaven.

Now we really must get to the bottom of this!

In Florida.

Happy times with my Grandsons.

*Let's leave the negatives
until tomorrow -*

*We will just deal with the
positives today.*

Chapter Seven

The Pride & The Passion
The Football Years

~ Chapter Seven ~

The Pride and The Passion:

The Football Years

My showroom on the Barking Road was a stone's throw from the home of West Ham United Football Club at Upton Park, albeit a rather long throw. Like many eastenders, I started going regularly to the matches on Saturdays but always made sure I left before the final whistle to ensure I was back in the showroom as the crowds filed past on their way home. I can say with some certainty that more than a few West Ham fans bought cars from Jack Petchey.

I owned a season ticket for many years and got to know many people through my time there but none more important than Brian Cearns, one of the Directors. My first meeting with Brian was not at Upton Park but at Wanstead Squash Courts where I was a member, he being the brother of the owner, Mabel. Through another member I showed interest in buying the squash courts and Brian negotiated on behalf of his sister. We didn't manage to agree terms and subsequently it was Brian who eventually bought them. From then on we became friends, socialising frequently until 1972 when he pulled me to one side and asked if I wanted to become a Director of West Ham United Football Club. This was a dream come true for a fan like myself and I didn't need to consider it for more than a second. My friendship with Brian grew and we could often be found after board meetings in the Old Friends Chinese Restaurant in Poplar.

Brian suffered with cancer for many years. In his last days he was told by the doctors that they were going to stop his blood transfusion and that he would die within 24 hours. He asked for the blood transfusion to be continued until he had seen his wife, Jackie, to say goodbye. I was also called to his bedside where he appointed me trustee and said his farewells. He was a good, true friend, and I've missed him greatly over the years.

I could see that the Club needed a healthy cash flow and spent many an hour at management meetings with the Commercial Managers - and West Ham was the first club to have mascots who paid to walk onto the pitch - how the young lads loved to walk on to the cheer of the crowds, having been given the honour as, maybe, a birthday present by their parents.

Brian Blower, the Commercial Manager, remembers several occasions when my support was needed when the Board were doubting the wisdom of investing in such matters as using advertising boards around the pitch (including replacing the half time score boards) and a telephone system whereby all direct enquiries on the Information Line would net the club a fee - culminating in quite a substantial income for the club.

On another occasion the Chairman, Len Cearns, objected to a young man in the Directors' Lounge because he was wearing jeans! Brian had to advise him that the young man was no other than pop star David Essex, who wore nothing BUT jeans - and probably very expensive ones at that - and having him there would be extremely good publicity! He's still a regular at West Ham!

Brian often used to laugh at the fact that I regularly used the restaurants at West Ham, and inspected all the public toilets at the ground - it was the only way I could satisfy myself that the facilities were good for our loyal supporters.

It would have been my ideal to have become Chairman of West Ham United but it was not to be, so I made the - maybe wrong - decision of leaving my Directorship behind and purchasing Watford FC from Elton John in 1990. It never reached the news - Saddam Hussein decided to pick that very day to invade Kuwait, which far overshadowed home news. Buying into Watford was not the best move I have ever made - I don't believe I was ever truly accepted by either the team, the staff, or the fans - particularly the fans - no matter what you did, you were wrong! Due to the disaster at Hillsborough, all football clubs were directed to build new all seating stands and we erected a wonderful new stand - but this was not enough to keep the fans happy. Neither was signing up Graham Taylor as Manager - although it placated them for a while.

Eddie Plumley, CE, myself & Elton John at Watford FC

Believe me, being a football chairman is not as glamorous as it sounds and I was more than happy - no relieved - to hand back the reins to Elton John when he felt able to take the club back.

Football did, however, introduce to me to handful of people who have remained good friends and are worthy of a mention. David Webb I've known for most of his life - from the days when we both lived in Chigwell when he would steal hub-caps from my car and try to sell them back to me, right through to his playing and managing career.

Former England Under 21's Manager, Peter Taylor, ran a football course at Clube Praia da Oura some years back and Glenn Roeder visits me frequently, probably due to our mutual 'positive thinking' attitudes.

Brian Blower, ex West Ham Commercial Manager, reminisced *"In 1983 I went with Jack Petchey and John Lyall (the Club Manager) to study the running of football in the USA and stayed at the Bay Harbour Hotel, Tampa, Florida for three nights. On our second night we came across a room crammed full of friendly hillbillies - at least 12 people! We were invited into the room for some home brewed hooch - there were kids sleeping in the bath, others in beds and then others wherever they could find space! It transpired that one of the family had booked some 6 months in advance, requesting a ground floor room - arrived on the due date - collected the room key - and let the rest of the very large family into the room through the window! At the time of hearing this Jack was busy making notes - no doubt to send to his hotel managers in Portugal - "Beware of Hillbillies booking ground floor rooms!"*

I'm now back in the stands supporting West Ham at their home matches, along with several members of my family. As they say - home is where the heart is - and mine is, without doubt, in the East End!

Life is a gift!

*All of us - who have the
ability - have the
responsibility to give
something back in life.*

Chapter Eight

A Life on the Ocean Wave

~ Chapter Eight ~

A Life on the Ocean Wave

During one of my spells of nervous exhaustion, prior to having discovered Dale Carnegie, I looked - on doctor's orders – for ways to relax. One came in the way of the Ilford Vapour Baths and it was there that I met a good friend named Joe Madden who introduced me to cruises. Along with his wife Freda, Joe was a frequent visitor to Madeira and knowing of my current problems invited Di and myself along for the holiday my doctor had long been advising me to take.

Such was my state of mind at the time that I had a sudden panic attack when meeting them both at Waterloo station. Joe arrived with not only his wife but with another young lady and I suddenly worried that my wife would somehow think I had arranged it – however it turned out to be Freda's daughter who had simply tagged along to say goodbye.

We joined the MV Venus at Southampton, where I was informed that it was known as the 'Vomiting Venus' and soon discovered why when we travelled through the Bay of Biscay. Steadily all of the passengers went down with sea sickness and I was among the last to succumb. I went back to my cabin where I called for a stewardess, when she arrived I told her of my ailment and she gave me some pills,

The MV Venus - better known to us as the "Vomiting Venus"

which she instructed had to be inserted in my anus! Not being incredibly well educated, as an inexperienced traveller and having never come across the word "suppository" I asked her where exactly I should put them. Much to my embarrassment as well as hers she explained. It was probably a good job that I felt so ill! During this trip to Madeira, Joe and Freda went to the beach but I went to Blandy's, the shipping agent, and canvassed for passengers getting off the ship at Southampton, for the car hire business, this being another classic example of never being able to completely leave my work behind.

I could tell you many a tale about Joe and myself and the things we got up to in those days. I recall that we had docked at a foreign port – which one, I fail to remember. We found ourselves in a nightclub where Joe was dancing with a girl. I too joined in the revelry and when Joe came back to the bar I was away on the dance floor. Joe thought I had left. When I got back to the bar the clubs 'heavies' presented me with a massive bar bill, which I simply couldn't pay. After much 'discussion' I thought I was about to be clumped, but rather than that they took all my money and threw me off the premises, leaving me to walk back to the ship. When I returned Joe was fast asleep and was snoring his head off. I woke him immediately and told him of my predicament. "You didn't pay?" he asked. "Yes" was my reply to which Joe responded "Oh you don't do things like that, I went down to the toilet and out the back window!"

On another occasion we went skiing in Vengens. We went down to the village and returned by train. During the journey we met two ladies, had a great laugh and may have been a bit saucy to them, even if they were 'big strong girls'. They understood little English but enough to know that we were taking the mickey out of them for being so big and strong. The next morning we booked in to have a massage. Upon arrival who were our masseurs? – none other than the 'big strong girls! Needless to say they gave us a pretty hard time!

In 1998 Joe claimed he received the OBE, being the joker he is. He later admitted that was because he was now "Over Bloody Eighty!"

Joe and I would meet regularly at the steam baths with other friends – Jim Green, Jim Suthers, Ron Tyrell, Edgar Pratt, Les Sutton, Harry French and Will Lintonbon. Each week Jim Green would arrange a collection, eventually developing enough funds to buy a new small bus for the handicapped scouts, which we presented at Baden Powell House. From that time onwards we have always been committed to helping the handicapped scouting fraternity.

Another friend, Keith Sterling, and I sailed one year on what was known as an "educational cruise". Our education was more or less confined to extending our knowledge of drinks, and increasing our capacity in this direction! During the day we often got roped in to play deck hockey or some other healthy pursuit for which we were totally unsuitable – and on trips ashore we would visit ruins that were in even worse conditions than ourselves!

Two weeks of this jollity were usually enough and one trip down the African coast, there was another week to go and we decided that we'd had enough and wanted to avoid the Bay of Biscay at all costs. So we made enquiries about flying home from our last port of call, Casablanca. Apparently cruise ships have special, cheaper port dues than other ships, and a condition imposed by the authorities is that passengers must return to the ship and not break their journeys unless there are "exceptional circumstances". So, undaunted, we devised a plot whereby a telegram would be sent on the day before we arrived in Casablanca, to the effect that "Uncle Bert" had died and that we were expected back for the funeral – urgently.

We were duly summoned to the Purser's office – to be greeted by an ashen faced Officer who, before saying anything, insisted that I had a drink and sat down. He was clearly distressed at being the bearer of bad news, and blurted out "Uncle Bert's dead" – and waited for my reaction. So there was I – confronted by a weeping Purser – trying to keep a straight face – so trying to keep sincere, I answered with absolute truth "It wasn't entirely unexpected". We flew home from Casablanca.

Now something of an intrepid seaman - and thoroughly enjoying a life on the ocean wave, I took my children to the Boat Show. My youngest daughter, Amanda Jane felt ill, and one of the owners of a stand of boat-builders was particularly kind, giving Amanda a seat and a glass of water, and generally making her feel a lot less conspicuous than she had been. While Amanda was settling herself, I looked casually over one of the boats on the stand, not particularly having any interest in buying it - but the boat builder was so kind and helpful that I decided, on impulse - very unusual for me - to buy the boat - which was ready for immediate delivery - also unusual at that time. Of course, it had to be named "Amanda Jane". My wife,

Di, wouldn't come out on the water but I talked all four children into sailing at weekends - my son, John, being the most regular and enthusiastic - he sailed with me a lot, together with Mike Jennings, an experienced sailing friend who I played squash with. Of course, in time, the novelty wore off - and the maintenance required was too much for my novice boating experience, and I decided to cut my losses and stick to the larger type of vessels - cruise liners - which, of course, require no ongoing work! My daughter Susan's husband, Ray, was more than keen to sail, but unfortunately turned out to be a particularly bad sailor - even now he goes green every time he gets within 6 feet of a motor vessel!

As well as the ocean, I have been found from time to time on the River Thames, mostly while throwing riverboat parties. If I recall correctly the 'Jock' and the 'Silver Barracuda' played host to the various themed costume parties that I threw annually for friends, family and business acquaintances. In fact, I had arranged a party on the "Jock" on the very evening that I was voted a Director of West Ham United Football Club. For the first time ever, I had to leave a friend, Joe Egan, in charge of greeting my guests at the party, although I managed to join them in good time for the "off".

Among the many themes, I can remember there were Country and Western, Pirates, World War Two, Pantomime, Caribbean and most notably a Roaring Twenties event, in which I clearly recall all

One of our first boat parties - aboard The Jock

my guests roaring with laughter when an American Sales Manager – Lonnie Brooks Munch III (yes, really!) – arrived in a 1920s striped woollen bathing suit complete with straw boater and bare feet! He caused quite a stir among the general public on the South Bank of the Thames, I can tell you - added to the fact that he lived in Kensington, so heaven only knows what his fellow tube passengers must have thought.

The Silver Barracuda also played host to my seventieth birthday party in which I made a speech stating that I only wanted to see three more birthdays - my 80th, my 90th and my 100th. Laughter followed a loud gasp, but the thing I found most funny, was that they thought I was joking!

My 80th birthday was celebrated in the same fashion and a wonderfully glorious day it was it too, the sun shone brightly and the Thames was lined

Note to self - secretary looking shabby, must speak to her.

Jack Petchey ..... alias .....

with Londoners basking in the heat and enjoying beverages at the many riverside cafes and bars. Many of my guests took some wonderful pictures from the boat that day; cruising up and down the Thames being a great way to see some of the impressive landmarks our nation's capital has to offer.

I am now nearing the time when we will start planning my 90th birthday celebrations – hopefully they will be bigger and better than ever before – after all, I've never been 90 before!

*Picture a world where
every young person
can dream great dreams
and live up
to their potential.*

Chapter Nine

Giving it all Back

~ Chapter Nine ~

Giving it all back:

The Jack Petchey Foundation

When my family was growing up, my sister Joan gave me something of a nickname that has stuck with me ever since – and it rings true more now than ever before. As a way of teaching my children the value of money, I would insist that if they wanted anything they would have to raise half the money and I would give them the other half; its now one of the main principles of the Foundation, and why my sister dubbed me "the Fifty-Fifty Man".

Plagued by back troubles that started whilst in the Navy, I finished up in the London Hospital, where the specialist advised me that my only option was to have an operation. I had two chances – the operation would be a success, or I may never walk again. Asking him – if he were I – what would he do? He replied that he wouldn't take a chance with the operation. I took his advice, but continued again and again to have back pain.

I later came under the care of Brian Roper – a specialist in Rheumatoid Arthritis and medical doctor for West Ham United Football Club. He treated me for several years, at one time admitting me to the King Edward VII Hospital for Officers & Gentlemen – although how, I will never know, as I was neither an Officer nor a Gentleman!

During this stay in hospital I was drugged for seven days to stop me moving and experiencing any pain, and after this time I was lowered into their swimming pool – it was sheer heaven! This experience led me to head a team to fund and install a hydrotherapy pool at the London Hospital. One of our fund-raising activities was to run Greyhound Racing Nights at the Walthamstow Stadium, which was great fun, having several celebrities like Warren Mitchell, AKA Alf Garnet helping with the cash collections.

I also attended Brian's Harley Street surgery where one day his nurse was manipulating my back. All of sudden she screamed out "Brian, I've got it, I've got it" – and he rushed in to find that she had "popped" a vertebrae back into place. Since then I've had very little pain.

During my years at Clube Praia da Oura, I was shown around two children's homes, the Casa dos Pirilampos and Gaivota. Unfortunately the Portuguese government does not fund such institutions and they rely on charitable donations. Since 1977 the children from the two homes have enjoyed parties thrown at the Clube for them, and for the past ten years or so have participated in their own Achievement Award schemes, being nominated for effort or excellent behaviour. The funds have been used to buy a television, video, educational cassettes, books and computer equipment.

Seeing the children at these two homes reminded me of the days when I used to throw open the gardens of my home in Chigwell to children from the Handicapped Scouts group, and Dr. Barnado's at Barkingside. There was great frivolity, lots of noise and excitement, and they all left clutching 'goody bags'. Whenever I passed Dr. Barnado's, the kids would wave and clap, and it never, ever failed to bring a lump to my throat.

Having donated to various charities close to my heart over the years, I decided to set up a Foundation. I felt that the area in which I had lived and worked all my life had given me a lot and now it was time to give it back – big time!

In 1998 my secretary was handling the main body of work involved but had many other duties of her own so I concluded that it would be better to put this into the hands of someone with the relevant experience who could devote his energies into forming a full time "company" for the work, which I anticipated would grow tremendously. Without one man in particular the Foundation may never have grown into what it is today nor have been as successful. I knew that I wanted to help more young people in the London and Essex areas but to fully achieve all I had in mind I would need someone with dedication and experience. Here Andrew Billington explains how he came to be the man to fit the role:

"I first met Jack Petchey in the early 1990's. At the time I was Chief Executive of a charity called Winged Fellowship (now renamed Vitalise). Winged Fellowship provides holidays and respite care for people with disabilities and one centre, Jubilee Lodge, was based at Chigwell in Essex. Jack Petchey kindly agreed to support this work with a donation.

In 1998 I had been Chief Executive for 10 years and was wondering about my next role. This coincided with Jack Petchey thinking about how he would like to do more for the community and young people particularly. (He had already supported a number of groups informally, ably assisted by his PA Barbara Staines).

Jack wrote to me in July 1998 asking whether I would help him establish a grant making trust and then run it for him. I said that if he wanted to do that he really needed to set up a foundation and register it with the charity commission with trustees. Jack replied saying that he felt this was a bit bureaucratic and he liked to do things simply so there was no further correspondence until the autumn when he wrote again saying that he had given the matter further thought and was prepared to establish a "formal" Foundation.

From November 1998 I worked on a part-time basis from home while doing consultancy work for other charities.

The Jack Petchey Foundation was formally established in August 1999 and I moved to

Exchange House in Ilford to work alongside Jack and Barbara Staines in establishing and developing the work. The priority right from the start was that the Foundation should benefit young people aged 11~25. Initially we focussed on East London and West Essex but over the coming years this geographical area grew to include all London boroughs and the whole of Essex.

Before joining Jack, I had spent 20 years working in charities, sometimes as a fundraiser, so it was a very new experience for me to reverse my role to giving money away rather than asking for it. Having been a fundraiser however helped me to understand some of the issues and problems faced by charities."

With Andrew at the helm we started work. The key aim of the Foundation right from the early days was to support programmes that benefited young people to enable them to grow in confidence and contribute to society. It was agreed that this should mainly be done through youth organisations and schools.

I also stuck to my tried and trusted regime of "meeting half way – you find half, I give half". The Achievement Award Scheme, on the other hand, worked on a different basis with schools, clubs and uniformed organisations being invited to partake in the scheme where one member would be proposed monthly to win £200 to be spent within their group. The award winner did not necessarily have to excel,

I thoroughly enjoy speaking with the kids!

but they had to have made a significant endeavour or effort within the club. Not everyone can excel, but everyone can try. By the end of that first year 1,140 awards were handed to schools, clubs, uniformed organisations and countless other participants. Award winners are encouraged to aim higher and higher and judged more on their determination to succeed. I firmly believe that this motivates young people more than if they are judged simply by their academic or sporting prowess.

By the Year 2000, the number of awards had doubled to well over to 2,400 and we decided to celebrate the turn of the century by setting aside £1 million for Millennium Awards. 332 organisations applied for a share and 141 were successful. On 18th January the following year the Awards were

My loyal band of 'helpers'.

presented at the first of our grand presentations at the London Planetarium with Tony Banks MP and Stephen Timms MP being the VIPs on this particular night to give out the awards and motivate the young people. Since then we've been lucky enough to have such prestigious guests as Sir Trevor Brooking, Chris Tarrant, Frank Bruno, Dame Kelly Holmes, Cheryl Baker, Ben Shepherd and Graham Norton as well as many Olympians, Paralympians, Government Ministers, senior Police Officers, sportsmen, musicians and even a Prince or two!.

The next presentation was held at the same location in July and featured former World Heavyweight Boxing Champion Frank Bruno and former England, West Ham United and F.A Cup winning footballer Sir Trevor Brooking, which caused extreme excitement amongst the award winners.

Since then the presentations have got bigger and better over the years with more prestigious guests and performances from young people from schools and clubs. Performances have covered just about every form and style of dance and music, drama, magic, gymnastic displays, drumming and drill as well as cheerleaders and majorettes! We even once had a champion trick footballing team who amazed the crowd! Many of our young performers have gone on to professional careers in the arts and some have even found fame and fortune through the wealth of TV talent shows currently in existence!

For me to list all the presentations and the

wonderful events we have seen over the years would be a book in itself – in fact one day, you never know, that book may get written – watch this space!

*In **very** good company!*

We later introduced the Leader Award Scheme for teachers, group leaders and organisers, which worked similarly to the Achievement Awards, but giving additional funds.

The key to the increasing number of participants was Andrew and his team who forged links with many charities including London Youth, Community Links and the Essex Association of Boys Clubs, who were among the key recipients of grants.

Now the Achievement Awards scheme has grown immensely and each Borough has a yearly award presentation, which includes entertainment by the young people of the borough, with much pride clearly shown by the youth involved - not to mention their parents.

The Foundation has grown in size now too – with fourteen full time staff. It gives me the greatest pleasure to see all the staff contributing their time and energies on these evenings, which, they tell me, they enjoy so much.

My partner, Frances Segelman, a well known sculptor, has been a wonderful supporter of the works that the Foundation does, and has used her considerable talents to sculpt busts of Her Majesty The Queen Elizabeth II, Prince Philip, the Duke of Edinburgh and many celebrities, which have been presented at the fund-raising dinners. Frances has also been responsible for introducing me to the world of art and culture – whilst I, in turn, have introduced her and her family to the power of positive thinking – Frances has said that the house has been a No Negative Speaking Zone for several years!

"Her Majesty Queen Elizabeth II"

As the Foundation has grown, I have had the great pleasure of hosting events in many prestigious locations – St. James's Palace, the House of Lords, HMS Ark Royal and Buckingham Palace. Whoever would have thought that an East End kid would sit down to dine with royalty, the Admiral of the Fleet and Members of Parliament?

In the company of two lovely ladies, HM Queen Elizabeth II and sculptor Frances Segelman

The Foundation has also enabled 76 schools to gain Specialist School Status, with donations totalling over £3M to enable them to do this. Project grants and training schemes also play a large part in the work the Foundation does – with the training of youth workers, who in turn play a large part in motivating young people, and encouraging them to play a useful role in society.

The primary focus of the Foundation is young people but we haven't always stuck by the letter of the law when it comes to assisting others. We have, for instance, helped the St. Francis Hospice in Havering-atte-Bower, and also the

Sampson Street Hospital for the elderly in Plaistow. However, we do try to keep within the boundaries of our criteria.

In 2008 Trudy Kilcullen took on leadership of the Jack Petchey Foundation at a time when we were refocusing our priorities. Trudy came with a background in charity management and had worked with young people as a youth worker and counsellor. She says *"One of the most amazing aspects of the Jack Petchey Foundation for me was the way it impacted on young people's self confidence and belief. Young people know the Foundation, they feel personally connected and when they receive an award their new found confidence enables them to go forward and achieve more. We come across endless stories giving examples of how a young person's life has been transformed. Jack's values and beliefs are core to the work of the Foundation. The whole focus is on helping young people to know "If I think I can I can.*

It really isn't about the money. Jack sees himself as 'investing' in young people, 'investing in the future'. On many occasions, he has asked me to stop making reference to the money that has been given and focus on the message!"

I set up the Foundation to support young people and to give them opportunities they may not otherwise have. I have come to realise that the MOST important message to get across is one of self belief. Every one of us is a unique individual, every one of us has something unique to offer to the world and what we have to do is find that passion, believe in ourselves, set goals, work hard and we will achieve.

Young people tell me that my story inspires them, if I can do it, they feel they can do it too! It doesn't matter about your background, what matters is your attitude. If we think negative then we will see negativity, if we think positive then we will see positivity. We create the world we want to see! That is one of the reasons I struggle with our media in this country. They generally give young people a knocking, so society comes to believe that young people are thugs. One of the things I hope that the Foundation can do is to challenge that perspective and highlight the great contribution that young people can and do make to our society.

It is important to me we don't single out or label different groups either. I remember a very kind teacher who discreetly passed me by when collecting the milk money so as I wouldn't be highlighted as 'disadvantaged' or 'poor'. All our programmes are universal programmes. We make sure we do our best to reach those who may have less opportunity or advantages but we don't single them out.

You never know the impact that a little bit of support can have. In the early days of our work the Foundation gave bursaries to young people who would have struggled to support themselves through professional training in youth work. We helped a

young man who couldn't afford to go to college to
train as a youth worker. Recently, almost ten years
later he wrote back *"I grew up in East London and
unfortunately saw many of my peers steer in the
wrong direction of crime, drugs and gangs. Many
ended up dead, in jail or mentally ill from all the
drugs they smoked. My fate seemed doomed as my
grades at school were less than desirable to say the
least. I got the opportunity to volunteer as a youth
worker on a notorious estate and also to study youth
work at the YMCA George Williams College.
Unfortunately I did not have any spare cash to pay
for the student fees. I reluctantly denied the
application but was told by the college of a Jack
Petchey Grant. I couldn't believe that someone
would give me money and not want anything back!
That day I made a promise to myself that when I
completed my studies I would pay back all the
money and also as a sign of my appreciation I
would contribute my time to do whatever task
deemed helpful.*

*It will be a full ten years this year since I first
received the grant and throughout that time I have
gained a BA (Hons) Degree in youth & community
studies. I have also worked as a senior manager in
several youth centres around the London boroughs
where my work has had a great impact on hundreds
of children and young people. I will always
remember that it all started with that 50% you gave
me and I am for ever grateful.*

I know the money I give back is not going to

make a huge difference to the hundreds of millions your business has acquired, but it is a promise I made and I wish to honour it".

It is just that sort of chain of giving that I would like to create. It gives me a lot of joy to see that sort of legacy for the future. Of course, I told him I didn't want the money back, I wanted him to think about how he, in turn, could invest that to help others and create his own chain of giving. Together we all create a better world.

Among the many events we now run is the Jack Petchey Speak Out Challenge. Working alongside Speakers Trust, an organisation dedicated to training the art of public speaking, the Challenge now trains over 15,000 young people each year from schools across London and Essex to take part in the country's biggest public speaking event. I am a great believer in the ability to speak well. When I first started in business I quickly realised the importance of making your points with confidence. Most young people today hold strong views and feel passionate about them. Our challenge gives them the opportunity to express themselves clearly and without fear. I really look forward to hearing the young people speak on a wide range of subjects every time the Speak Out Challenge comes around.

The Foundation now runs multiple events and takes part in many others that we do not necessarily organise. Here Lee Thompson, our Head of Events, talks about two that are close to all our hearts - Glee and the Lord Mayors Show.

Launch of the Speak Out Challenge in 2011

"The Jack Petchey Foundation has always been a great supporter of arts projects – the skills the arts teach young people - confidence, teamwork, self-discipline and expression are all things that the Foundation wants to actively encourage. The popularity of the American TV series Glee was the perfect opportunity for us to provide a programme that offered education and training in many different performing arts skills – dance, vocals and stage performance. The Jack Petchey Glee Club Challenge is a competition to find the best Glee club in London and Essex. It is a competition with a 1st, 2nd and 3rd place but, just as importantly, is an opportunity for us to provide training through a series of workshops and boot camps.

Now in its third year, the Challenge has had a huge impact on those taking part. The increase in confidence and skills of the performers has been outstanding. It is heartening to see that the competition means so much to all of those participating. The workshops have brought them into contact with musical theatre industry professionals who have been able to coach, guide and coax their performances. The Regional Finals, held at theatres across London and Essex, have seen sold out houses offering massive (and very loud) support to the groups taking part and the Grand Final has offered a unique opportunity to perform at high profile venues (including the Savoy Theatre and IndigO2).

With the support of celebrity patrons and judges Graham Norton, Tamzin Outhwaite and Brenda Edwards the programme has gone from strength to strength. The feedback from all those taking part has been extraordinary and it is clear, in some cases, that the experience has been life changing. From the outset, the Jack Petchey Glee Club Challenge was never intended to just be a competition – our aim was to prove that the best way to motivate young people was to push them to do better, get them to work as a team and encourage them along the way using the arts as a vehicle. It has been a great success and long may it continue.

One of my favourite events is The City of London Lord Mayor's Show which has been in existence for almost 800 years and is the largest unrehearsed street parade in the world. With 3 miles of floats, 500,000 spectators on the streets of London and millions watching live on BBC One it was inevitable that the Jack Petchey Foundation should become involved in the procession. Participating in

*the Lord Mayor's Show is genuinely a once in a
lifetime opportunity for our young people so, since
the Foundation's first entry into the Parade in 2007,
we have concentrated on involving as many young
people as possible. Thousands of young people
have taken part – we have produced bands,
gymnastic displays, buses, assorted floats, dance
groups and circus acts! Hours have been spent
rehearsing the young participants and all have done*

Lord Mayor's Show 2012

*a brilliant job. The route of the procession is over 3
miles – expecting a 12 year old girl to dance for that
distance is a huge ask. The marvellous thing about
our entries into the Lord Mayor's Show is the sheer
dedication, commitment and drive of the young
people.*

*In 2010 we had over 300 young people
participating – one of the floats consisted of 150
young people carrying the flags of every country that
has a language spoken in London. On that day it
rained like I have never seen before – within*

minutes everyone was soaked to the skin. However, not a single young person dropped out or moaned – in fact, they pulled themselves up and tried twice as hard. Their efforts shone through the rain. I don't think I have ever been prouder.

The Lord Mayor's Show also offers a great opportunity to get coverage of our young people on live national TV. We have been very fortunate in the coverage received, and the BBC have been very supportive. Many young people have been interviewed en route as well as Jack himself – a brilliant way to get the message across about how great our young people are!"

Another programme I love is Step into Dance. This is our partnership with the Royal Academy of Dance to bring professional after school dance classes to young people who may not otherwise have the opportunity to dance. I believe we deliver the programme in 200 schools, including over 50 special schools.

It is a real joy to see the thrill that young people get from working together to express themselves through dance. I have to say the standards are very high and the creativity of the performances is amazing. Sue Goodman, the programme lead, is one of the most dedicated people I have met and she really brings the best out of the youngsters. We have had young male street dancers who were about to be excluded from school before they got engaged in the programme and found something they were passionate about that focussed their energy. We have also given opportunity to young people with special needs to perform alongside their able bodied peers. The relationships that have formed through this are really quite special and I love the way the youngsters support each other whatever their ability – all are willing to 'give it a go' and that, in my mind, is what it is all about.

The Panathlon Challenge is a programme that really touches me. They deliver sports coaching and competitions to young people with special needs. Without this I understand there is no formal inter - school sports structure that will involve all the youngsters whatever their disability. The enthusiasm, determination and joy on the faces of the young people often moves me to tears. To see a young man who can only move his finger on a wheelchair joystick focussed on getting across that winning line is a reminder to all of us that if you really believe you can achieve – you will!

In 2011 I wanted to find a way to promote Table Tennis. When I was a youngster I used to get hours of fun out of a game of table tennis with friends. It is such a versatile game, can be played almost anywhere by anyone and adds a focus to ones 'free time'. The English Table Tennis Association came up with a plan to get table tennis equipment into schools and create a competition structure that linked in with the English Schools Table Tennis Association matches. So the London Schools Table Tennis Challenge was founded.

Each year 200 indoor and up to 40 outdoor tables have been placed in schools. The tables have created quite a focus with after-school and dance and lunchtime clubs springing up as well as table tennis being taught as part of the PE curriculum. It is a great form of exercise and focus and I hope young people will get a great deal out of learning the sport.

Other initiatives led by youth organisations but supported through grant making by the Jack Petchey Foundation include major grants such as:

TS Jack Petchey - The Foundation gave £1million for this sail training ship for the Sea Cadets, launched in July 2009. It trains young people across the UK in sailing skills as a route to developing self-confidence, teamwork and self-discipline.

Scouts Lodge at Gillwell Park - £1 million was invested in a new residential block to enable

scouts from across the South East to undertake self-development programmes.

Out of School Hours Programmes - Approximately £5 million has been given to support "Out of School Hours" programmes across London and Essex. These programmes have given young people 'somewhere to go and something to do', developing new interests and skills outside school.

The Petchey Centre for Entrepreneurship - To create opportunity, stimulate the development of an entrepreneurial approach and give people in East London a helping hand to get their business ideas off the ground, a grant of £500,000 was given to University of East London to develop this centre.

Summer Uni London - Grants totalling £1.5 million have been made to enable a range of summer activities for young people to be delivered across London in the school holiday period.

This is just a snapshot of our activity. Millions

of pounds have also been invested in grass roots youth projects. We have supported thousands of young people through funding overseas/community projects, young homeless hostels, environmental projects, performing arts, sports, training schemes, mentoring and counselling programmes as well as nearly all the uniformed youth organisations in London and Essex including Army Cadets, Police Cadets, Sea Cadets, Air Cadets, Scouts, Guides, Boys Brigade, Girls Brigade and St John Ambulance.

During the latter part of 2010 my son, John, fell ill. At first he had flu like symptoms, but as time went on he failed to respond to any treatment, and rapidly lost his energy levels. The family doctor sent him for tests, and it was discovered that he had a problem relating to his blood cells and needed frequent blood transfusions in order for him to function properly. After extensive hospital tests he was diagnosed in February 2011 with Myelodysplaic Syndrome, which to the layman is a severe, aggressive form of leukaemia for which there is no known "cure" – other than receiving a bone marrow transplant.

This news was quite a shock for the family, who all responded quickly by being tested to become possible bone marrow donors, but to our dismay, not one family member was found to be a match. So John went on the Bone Marrow list with the Anthony Nolan Trust – and we all kept our fingers well and truly crossed for him. He was lucky … a donor was found … and in July, only 5 months after being given the bad news, he received the transplant he badly needed.

The gift of life is the most precious gift that we would want to be able to give another. When I realised that it is relatively easy to donate bone marrow but found out just how hard it is to find a suitable match I felt that we had to do something to increase the chances of others finding help too.

I was surprised that there wasn't an official government led bone marrow donor programme like there is for blood donors. Without one inspirational mother (Shirley Nolan) who founded the Anthony Nolan Bone Marrow Register in 1974 when her own young son was in need of a bone marrow transplant, there simply wouldn't be a register in the UK. I found out that the Anthony Nolan Trust had a backlog of tissue samples to process and add to the register and that they especially wanted to recruit young people to join the register because they make better donors and increase the chance of a successful match.

So the Jack Petchey Foundation agreed to get involved! It was the beginning of a relationship that saw us enable over 11,000 tissue samples to be processed and added to the register and joined us in a 'mission' to get young people signed up.

Hardeep Singh Kohli, a radio and television presenter helped lead our joint 'Man on a Mission' campaign and in the course of a month we signed up a further 1343 new young donors.

Obviously the Jack Petchey Foundation wants young people to play a full part in society. Signing up to donate their blood stem cells is one of the greatest things they can do, as they could help save somebody's life.

Every year we meet thousands of positive young people who want to make a difference to society. One of the frustrations was that many of these were keen to help and yet were under the official donor sign up age of 18. The Anthony Nolan Trust too recognised that this was a problem and thankfully they had the sense and foresight to review the donor sign up age. In 2012, the age was lowered to 16 years.

"Man on a Mission, Hardeep Singh Kohli with students of the Jack Petchey Academy".

In many ways our relationship with Anthony Nolan is a perfect match! We meet the enthusiastic young people who want to give something to society; they harness the young people's desire and offer a potential to save a life by signing up to the bone marrow register. We have therefore continued to help and encourage young people through supporting their 'Register and Be a Lifesaver Programme' and I hope that this will enable many lives to be saved in the future.

My Son John's life was saved thanks to the Anthony Nolan Trust and the excellent hospital care he received, including months of chemotherapy which took quite a toll on his body, and he is, unfortunately, now in the position of waiting on yet another list – this time for a kidney transplant, but we're all hopeful that he will receive good news soon!

The Foundation is proud to have made a difference to the lives of young people and I get many letters from young people telling me how the Foundation has helped them change their lives. Here are some quotes below:

"You are a big influence not only on me, but many other young people too. You not only notice what young people do, but you reward us for our effort and make us feel proud of what we've done".
Jodie

"If you think you can, you can" is one of my favourite quotes of yours Jack. It just goes to portray

the fact that you value and encourage the idea that people need to believe in themselves, and by believing in themselves they can accomplish many things that they never thought they could".
Maureen.

"I want to say THANK YOU for everything you have done, not just for me, but for every person that has been recognised by your organisation. By having the Jack Petchey Foundation you have influenced me to strive to do my best in everything I do and to never give up. You are a fantastic role model to all young people". **Hanifah**

"Jack, you are a true inspiration for all of us. To be honest when I won the Achievers Award it wasn't the money I raised that was the best part about the award, it was the fact that I felt recognised and appreciated for what I had done. From the Award I have been inspired to go further and help other people and to do more. The Jack Petchey Foundation has given young people everywhere a platform to show what they have done well in their lives and inspire all to reach their potential". **Jesse**

Believe me, its very humbling when I read these wonderful tributes!

More than anything I believe that people should think of others and give back to society, no matter how small an act of kindness or generosity, and I want young people to know that in giving, you also receive, and the world is a better place for it!

This emphasis on positive affirmation, self

belief, the willingness to make an effort and to give to others are key to the development of the work of the Jack Petchey Foundation.

Ultimately, the thing that makes me happiest is when a youngster tells me they get the message 'If I think I can - I can'. That is the legacy I want to leave, that is the little mark I hope to make on future generations who will be responsible for leading and developing our country, our world. When I finally go 'upstairs' and meet my maker, I want to be able to say "I made a difference".

*Success consists of doing
the common things
of life uncommonly well.*

Chapter Ten

Back To School

~ Chapter Ten ~

Back To School

In this day and age a good education is vital for any young person to succeed in life and the Jack Petchey Foundation works with over 700 secondary schools. When we first introduced our Achievement Award scheme, little did we know that one day we would take that step further and build our very own school!

In the year 2000 Andrew Billington (the Director of the Jack Petchey Foundation) and I were invited to Number 10 Downing Street (an honour in itself) where we were asked by the then Prime Minister, Tony Blair, Andrew Adonis and Lord Levy to discuss the possibility of sponsoring an Academy in east London.

With the Achievement Award and Leaders Award schemes in place and the successful sponsoring of the production of school planners, Andrew and I agreed that this was an opportunity not to be missed.

After much deliberation and planning, a site in Hackney was chosen. Early in the process we looked at the Mossbourne site but Sir Clive Bourne was already in early discussions with the Learning Trust so we decided against that site and selected another. At the time the site was home to the Kingsland

Comprehensive School which was struggling with poor examination results. The buildings were in drastic need of repair and some were completely unsuitable. There was much debate as to whether the Kingsland School should be refurbished or knocked down; it was deemed far more sensible and practical to begin again with a new purpose built school.

It would be the rebirth of a site that over years had seen many changes. Just 200 metres away on the other side of Cecilia Road, there used to be a river called Hackney Brook, a tributary of the River Lea... it was not a trickle... when in flood it could be 70-100 feet wide during the 19th century!

It is thought that nearby Kingsland Road was originally a Roman road. The site's address is Shacklewell Lane and the word Shacklewell was first mentioned in records in 1490 and means 'Spring at or near which animals were tethered' giving a hint at what it might have been like during the 15th century. The site had been used for many things over the years - in the 19th century there were domestic houses around the roads and in the middle there were greenhouses and a nursery. In 1894 there was a sawmill and printing works. It was in 1937 that a school was established as Dalston County School. This was renamed the Kingsland School in 1949 and later Kingsland Comprehensive School, and now we were to continue that legacy by demolishing it and building a brand new one - the

Petchey Academy.

Now Andrew and I, although enthusiastic and excited about the project, had absolutely no idea how to run a school, that job would have to go to someone with knowledge and experience and that person was David Daniels. We advertised for the first Principal in 2005 and David was appointed but the Academies Division at the DFES, as it was called then, did not allow us to proceed until after the General Elections held that year were over and the funding agreement signed. So David kindly worked 'at risk' for several months before a contract could be drawn up and signed.

In the beginning David had no office, administration support or even a school! However, he did have the satisfaction of working with almost a blank canvas to set up this new Academy. Not an easy task by any stretch of the imagination but one I am sure he found exciting and stimulating, not to mention challenging!

In September 2006 the first 180 students began their secondary school career in a temporary block on the Multi Use Games Area at the bottom of our site while the main building was completed. At that time there were 14 staff working hard with David on the mammoth task of building a school from the ground up ... literally.

An Academy Development Board existed until 2006 when responsibility transferred to the first Governing Body. The first Governing Body Meeting was held on 9th February 2006 and Andrew Billington was elected Chair. The Academy is an independent school funded by the Government specialising in Health, Care and Medical Sciences.

After much stress, hard graft and commitment from all involved, 2007 saw the completion of our shiny new building. September saw the Academy open its brand new doors to 360 students. It had cost around £34million mainly funded by the government but with £2million from the Jack Petchey Foundation.

Now in its 7th year, the Academy has grown way past our wildest expectations and we are all very proud of it. None more so than Olivia Cole, our current Head Teacher:

"The Petchey Academy's Latin motto is 'Excelsior' which succinctly captures our ambition for academic excellence in an environment where students are encouraged to develop their interests and talents in all areas. I strongly believe that the students are proud of their academy and value its unique character. Our sponsor, Jack Petchey, gives us that distinctive character. Both students and staff follow his maxim, "If I think I can, I can" which proves an apt guide for anyone striving for excellence in their studies, extra-curricular activities and working relationships.

Students have a clear set of moral values and a sense of responsibility towards the academy. Expectations of commitment to study, social responsibility and respect are encapsulated in our "Petchey Way". Ask any student what the "Petchey Way" means to them and answers will range from wearing smart uniform and holding doors open for people, to working hard for the highest qualifications and successfully winning a place at a top university.

The Academy is here to nurture and stimulate our students whatever their interests and ambitions. Whether they are fascinated by higher maths, music or politics, we encourage and support them to pursue their ambitions. If they are inspired by medical science, the Petchey Academy is the place for them. Our links and partnerships with teaching hospitals and universities, coupled with our Clinical Skills Lab create a stimulating environment to explore the possibilities".

The Academy may be named after me, but many people have helped it become what it is today - a school all can be proud of - myself, the staff at the Foundation, the board of governors, the faculty and, of course, the students for whom the school was built.

During a special assembly by the head teacher in October 2007 all students were asked if they knew what grew from acorns and were given a pouch with an acorn inside with the words:

"Jack Petchey and I hope that you will keep this pouch while you are at the Petchey Academy and that from time to time you will take out the acorn and ask yourself whether you are doing all you can to become the adult that you would like to become. Choose today what sort of person you want to be.

If you have not bothered to work hard in the past ... start now ... why not prove to yourself that you can

Planting the Jack Petchey Rose at the Petchey Academy.

If you want new friends, begin today to be a good friend ... don't hurt people with your words or actions but be friendly and helpful. Be a good friend and you will find many people want to be your friend.

Begin today to think about what sort of adult you would like to be. Nearly all the best jobs need qualifications… if you begin to work hard now it will be easier in the years to come."

One person who epitomises this philosophy and who deserves special mention is Andrew Billington. As you have read Andrew has been involved from the very start and has watched and helped our little acorn grow into a mighty oak tree. It is only fitting that Andrew has the last word.

"There is almost a palpable air of anticipation and excitement when Jack Petchey comes to the Academy. This awe and respect by students is well earned. The Academy bears his name; Jack has an established reputation in East London as an entrepreneur; he has the dignity, bearing and silver hair of a patrician and is older than most of their grandparents ... but more important than all this is that he is an East Londoner who has experienced some of the pressures and struggles that many of them face as they grow up and he understands the extra effort that has to be made by inner city young people to succeed. They are proud that Jack Petchey, their patron, remains actively interested in the Academy and his motto, mentioned earlier, is regularly repeated: ' If I think I can, I can'.

There was a 6 year period between the initial discussions at 10 Downing Street in 2000 and the arrival of the first 180 students in 2006. During this time there was much discussion about the values and priorities we wished to incorporate in a new school. Jack often talked about using the building and facilities to their full advantage. He is now pleased that there are 'out of school hours' activities every evening - sometimes to 10pm. The excellent gym is actively used by staff and the local community from 6.30 in the morning until well into the evening. At weekends there are extra lessons, sport activities, community meetings and even weddings.

Jack has played a key part in inviting celebrity guests to speak at assemblies and schools, to name other events. These have included John Bercow, the Speaker of the House of Commons; Baroness D'Souza, the Lords' Speaker; Lord Levy; Boris Johnson, Mayor of London; Jude Law, actor; Sir John Mills of the Olympics committee; Lord Low of Dalston; Ara Darzi, Baron of Denham, Lord Adonis, past Minister for Schools to name just some. We were pleased that the Right Hon. Ed Balls MP Secretary of State for Children, Schools and Families formally opened the Academy on 14th May 2006 when a time-capsule was buried in the grounds.

Jack Petchey, through his Foundation, has given valuable extra opportunities and equipment for students and staff at the Academy:

- A residential programme for all new 11 year old students, usually held at the Stubbers Centre in Essex in October. For many youngsters this is the first time they have been away from home and it plays an important part in cementing relationships between students and staff

- Out of school hours activities and 'booster sessions' on Saturdays

- Table tennis equipment and trampolines

- A minibus

- Christmas hampers for the staff

- Fruit for staff common rooms

- Assistance with overseas trips

- A reward programme for students

The academy also participates in the Achievement Award Scheme, Speak Out Challenge and Step into Dance programmes, all funded by the Foundation.

As I write this in 2013 the Academy has been open for 7 years. There are now over 1,000 students and 150 members of staff. There is a thriving 6th form called University Gateway. We are about to say goodbye to the first students who arrived in 2006 as they prepare to go to universities, some to the very best in the country.

The Petchey Academy, alongside other academies and schools in Hackney, has transformed opportunities for the young people in the Borough. Indeed, GCSE results that used to be among the worst in the country are now significantly above the national average.

What is even more important is that students are leaving school feeling more confident and better equipped to meet the complexities and challenges of adult life.

The School song captures the ethos of the Academy and Jack's vision for it:

This is our school, but it is more than that
This is the place that's making us the best we can be
We come to learn, but we come to grow as well
Together with our friends and community

Chorus
There's nothing we can't achieve
We'll tell you what we believe
In succeeding every day
We want to shout out loud
Because we are all so proud
That we do things the Petchey Way

We're out to win, we are going to show them all
That we understand team spirit, respect and playing fair
We can excel, we can be bold in our success
Having fun, feeling safe, and showing that we care.

It is quite possible that this Academy will turn out to be Jack's most significant legacy ... a real gift to the young people of East London ... his home, his community and his people".

Brick walls there will always be - but there is always a way through to the other side.

Chapter Eleven

Celebrations & Jubilations

~ Chapter Eleven ~

Celebrations and Jubilations

I find now, with the sentimentality that comes with advancing years, that I have a lot to celebrate and be thankful for. I have been blessed with four children, eight grand-children and six great grand-children.

There have been many milestones in my life – being given the Freedom of the City of London in 1980, for example and in 1999 I celebrated 50 years of business with a large party for friends and colleagues in the Dorchester Hotel. Once again my business had turned in a different direction; in a similar way to when I found that selling cars was easier than driving them, and selling showrooms was a quicker way to profit than selling cars – I discovered that investing in other people's property companies was far less management intensive than selling properties. We had amassed a property portfolio worth some £115M, but with that came a whole department of staff from managers to surveyors to secretaries and clerks. "Why do I need all this administration?" I thought to myself. "You don't – get someone else to do all the work". So we sold the vast majority of the portfolio to another large property conglomerate and set about investing! Of course, I then found myself with a department

Celebrating 50 years of business The Dorchester Hotel

full of Investment Managers, secretaries and clerks – I had come full circle! Some of the investments have been particularly good – others not so good – but its all part of the learning curve – and I have convinced myself that I am never too old to learn! During these latter years I have been awarded "Property Achiever of a Lifetime" followed swiftly by a "Lifetime Achievement Award" from the Variety Club "Props" in 2001. Not bad for an oldie, eh?

Clube Praia da Oura surpassed all expectations, winning accolade after accolade within the tourism industry, being labelled a Resort of International Distinction by RCI. However, in 2012 I felt it was time to hang up my "timeshare boots" and pass the company on, selling to the MGM Group who will no doubt take Clube Praia da Oura and all the resorts within the Petchey Leisure group to a bright new future.

In 2003 the University of East London recognised my efforts with an Honorary Fellowship, which came as a great surprise. My family were with me when I donned my gown and mortar board – those 79 years of study had paid off at long last! Now was the time to turn the tables on my grandson, who had recently graduated from Brunel University! I have also since received Honorary Fellowships at The University of East Anglia and Queen Mary University in East London. For a lad who never took an interest in either books or learning in school, this is some achievement, let me tell you!

It isn't every day that you have a rose named after you – but in 2003 St. Bonaventure's School in Forest Gate surprised me at one of the Foundation presentations with a "Jack Petchey" rose. Its scent is magnificent, and the petals dark red with a touch like velvet. I was quite choked as I stood on the

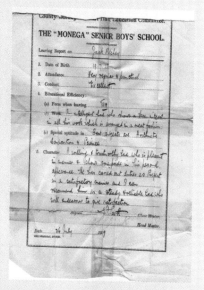

OK, so it took me a few years ... but I got there in the end!

Grandson Matthew at Brunel

stage – at a loss for words for once – my Mother's favourite flower was a rose, and how I wished she could have been there at that minute! Luckily the school had thoughtfully provided me with a rose bush for each member of my family, and they are now growing beautifully in all our gardens, and every time I pass, I think of Mum.

In June 2004 I celebrated 50 years in the Masons. A man by the name of Stan Duffield Jnr was the publican at the William the Conqueror on the Romford Road and his father Stan Snr ran the Blind Beggar public house in Mile End. They used my car services frequently and I became good friends with the pair of them and subsequently they proposed me into the Tillingbourne Masonic Lodge as a candidate.

I was initiated in 1954 which turned out be something of a nerve racking experience, despite having negotiated many business deals, I couldn't help but feel rather nervous and intimidated.

I progressed through various Masonic offices until I was installed as Master at the Roebuck Hotel in Buckhurst Hill. On that occasion the Tillingbourne Lodge had 109 people in attendance, including Lord Chelmer, a partner in E. Edwards Son and Noice, the firm of solicitors who have acted for me to this day.

Wally Sherwood, the then Lodge Secretary, died suddenly and Laurie Corbett – a very senior Mason – encouraged me to take on the Secretaryship of the lodge. I felt incredibly honoured to be asked but still had reservations as to whether I could cope.

I served as secretary for many years when I decided to pass on the opportunity to someone else and it gave me great pleasure to recommend and see accepted, Victor Stafford Newman, who had always been a great friend to me.

I was appointed as a Provincial Grand Steward and then made Provincial Grand Treasurer.

The Tillingbourne Lodge Secretaryship brought me in touch with the Essex Provincial powers-that-be and was co-opted onto the Charity Committee for the Essex Provincial Grand Masters Grand Charity which raised a tremendous amount of money for the Royal Masonic Institute for Boys.

I would like to make special mention of Col. A.R. Kiggins (or Bert to his friends) a Deputy Provincial Grand Master of Essex and my Masonic 'mentor' and guide, and shall always be appreciative of his guidance, kindness and help.

Looking back over all my years with the Masons I am sure that my membership and fellow members have helped me greatly in one way or another and for that I will always remain thankful.

On practically the same day that I celebrated 50 years as a Mason, I was honoured by Her Majesty the Queen, by being awarded the OBE for services to youth in East London and Essex. What an honour for an East End boy! My Mother – bless her, if she

thought she felt proud when she watched me on the Sunday morning Boy Scout marches, just think how her heart would have swelled with pride to think of my receiving a medal from the Queen!

This was followed by the CBE eight years later. Much was made of the fact that I chose not to have this honour presented by the Queen at Buckingham Palace, but for me it was a simple choice – I'd already received my OBE at the Palace with three of my family present, but this honour I chose to receive in front of the people I'd dedicated my charitable works to – the young people of London and Essex. The natural choice was that this should be at a scouting event – an organisation very close to my heart. So on 16th March 2012 at the Jack Petchey Achievement Award event for Scouts Greater London Middlesex West at the Great Hall, Kensington, I was presented with my CBE by the Lord Lieutenant of Greater London, Sir David Brewer CMG, on behalf of Her Majesty the Queen. Almost 800 people were in attendance including seven mayors, eight Representative Deputy Lieutenants, senior representatives from all of the UK's major youth organisations and, of course, my partner, Frances, my family, friends and members of my staff! The important aspect of the presentation was that it was made amongst all of the other awards being received by the young scouts that evening. It made a great picture – the ex-scout from East Ham now being made a CBE. Proof positive that "If you think you can – you CAN!" A wonderful evening, and I still occasionally watch it on YouTube, just to remind myself!

Of course, its not all been plain sailing, and I've learned lessons along the way. I don't know

Being awarded the CBE with my family present.

whether I have just been unlucky, or it's a reflection of the society we now live in – but I have experienced not one, but two house burglaries. The first one occurred – as most break-ins do – at night. Unfortunately I was in bed at the time and actually heard the burglar walk into the bedroom. I don't know what made me do it – but I leapt out of bed, wearing nothing other than my socks – grabbed something heavy and shouted at him – he legged it down the stairs with me in hot pursuit – I must have looked ludicrous! I certainly felt it when I realised what I looked like!

The other break in occurred after I had – in my infinite wisdom – left a spare front door key in the centre console of my car – and then went abroad. The car was broken into – and there was the house key! The thief then had the run of the house – which also included the keys to a friend's car which was also parked outside! Two security lessons learned in one hit – don't leave keys inside your car – and have a good security alarm and CCTV cameras installed around and inside the house! However, that's all part of life's rich tapestry, as they say!

I'm very lucky that I've been blessed with good friends, good mentors, good supporters and at almost nearly 90 – I try to keep active and on occasion go cycling with my Grandsons. One activity I can no longer participate in, and miss, is playing squash – or racquet ball – which was always an important part of my life. I loved the physical exercise, competition and the social aspect. I started playing at Wanstead Squash Club, and established some lifetime friends there – Dr. John Phillips and Brian Cearns to mention but two. I recall being taught by a "Khan" who stood at the side of the court, cigarette in mouth, hardly moving – and had me running all over the court. His examples of practice and discipline have been used over the years to help others who, needless to say, are now considerably better than me!

One of the biggest compliments I have ever received was from the Dale Carnegie Corporation. Having given away countless numbers of their books and recommending dozens of friends and colleagues to attend their courses, I was awarded the Dale Carnegie Leadership Award. Here's an extract from a letter received from Clive Thompson of Dale Carnegie London. *"Some of the last words from Mr Carnegie before he died were to his dear friend, Harry O Hamm, who was our licensed sponsor in Southern California – and they were "Keep my dream alive". Of all the people I know, there is no-one who is doing this more than you through your Foundation. On behalf of the Dale Carnegie Organisation we applaud and thank you. Stay well, Jack, and keep that Dale Carnegie book by your bedside".*

I'm very fortunate in having a great view of the Thames from my window, and nothing gives me greater pleasure than seeing, on occasion, the TS Jack Petchey sailing past, with its crew of Naval Cadets on a training "expedition". The Foundation commissioned the boat to help fulfil the potential of the Naval Cadets and young people of London and Essex, and moors on the Thames on occasion at HMS President, where it was officially launched.

2015 will see another celebration – my 90th Birthday! I'm going to make this one go with a bang! Having almost reached my tenth decade, I still enjoy the cut and thrust of business, and work every day, particularly as the profits we make can now be spent helping the youth of London & Essex to achieve something with their lives.

I hope I've made my Mother proud of me – she helped me considerably all those years ago – and I've tried to repay her in every way I could.

When fate hands you a lemon, make lemonade.

~ *TIMELINE* ~

1925	*19th July*	Born.
1937		Prosecuted at East Ham Magistrates Court for working under age.
1938		Left school & began work as an Office Boy at the Solicitors Law Stationery Society in Fetter Lane for 12s 6d per week.
1939	*3rd September*	Served as a Scout Police Messenger - on a bicycle for 2 years.
1941	*July*	Served as an Auxiliary Fire Service Messenger - on a motor cycle for 2 years.
1943	*17th May*	Niece, Jill Bateman, born.
1943	*9th August*	Volunteered to join the Royal Navy.
1944	*25th February*	Transferred to the Fleet Air Arm and became a Petty Officer Electrical Air Fitter until the end of World War II.
1944	*15th July*	Nephew, Michael Bateman, born.
1947	*17th January*	Discharged from the Fleet Air Arm and returned to work for the Solicitors Law Stationery Society.

1948		Decided to "go it alone" having been advised that he was "unsuitable for management". Bought an Armstrong Siddeley motor car - a bad buy - which was eventually returned. Bought another car, a Hudson Terraplane, with which he founded his first Car Hire business.
1949	**13th December**	Bought and sold on the same day - No. 48 Goldsmith Avenue, Manor Park, E12. (First property transaction).
1949	**25th November**	Married Diana Harrison.
1950	**4th May**	Daughter, Jacqueline Lesley, born.
1953	**9th July**	Daughter, Susan Ann, born.
1954		Initiated into the Tillingbourne Masonic Lodge.
1954		Embarked into the "property" business.
1957	**16th August**	Son, John Keith, born.
1963	**20th July**	Niece, Jeni Bateman, born.
1968	**3rd June**	Daughter, Amanda Jane, born.
1969	**October**	Was introduced to the idea of building a holiday complex in the Algarve, Portugal.
1970	**January**	CPO was "born".
1972	**2nd December**	Mother, Dorothy (Doll) died.

1972	June	Became a Director of West Ham United Football Club.
1974	April	Revolution in Portugal.
1974		"Almost" went bankrupt.
1974	12th January	Grandson, Nic Bruce, born.
1977	26th June	Grandson, Marc Bruce, born.
1980	25th January	Grandson, Matthew Rantell, born.
1980		Bought first computer for the company.
1980		Awarded the Freedom of the City of London.
1981	19th June	Grandson, Anthony Rantell, born.
1982		The idea of timeshare was made known to him in America and he took the idea to Clube Praia da Oura - since that day there have been c 18,000 satisfied owners at the resort & 28,000 owners in affiliated resorts.
1984	2nd November	Grandson, Andrew Rantell, born.
1984	March	Published the first CPO Newsletter, the Golden Beach News.
1988		Built the first bowling green in the Algarve at Clube Praia da Oura.
1990	July	Resigned as Director of West Ham United Football Club.

1990	August	Became Chairman of Watford Football Club.
1990	12th June	Grand-daughter, Lauren Petchey, born.
1994	June	Clube Praia da Oura received the RCI Hospitality Award.
1995	October	Admitted to the RCI "Timeshare Hall of Fame".
1996	September	Resigned as Chairman of Watford Football Club.
1996	9th December	Presented with the Property "Achievement of a Lifetime" Award.
1997	July	Bought the Oura Praia Hotel in the Algarve, Portugal.
1999	4th August	Jack Petchey Foundation founded.
1999	4th October	Celebrated 50 Years of Business.
1999	4th November	Presented with a plate by the Civil Governor of the Algarve, in recognition of his contribution to Algarve tourism.
2001	21st November	Received the Variety Club "Props" 2001 "Lifetime Achievement" Award.
2001	9th March	Great Grandson, Alfie Edward George Bruce, born.
2002	25th April	Received the "UK Property Entrepreneur of the Year" Award.

2003	**4th May**	Wife, Diana, died.
2003	**20th November**	Awarded an Honorary Fellowship of the University of East London.
2004	**1st January**	Jack Petchey Foundation - Portugal - founded.
2004	**11th May**	"Sponsor of the Year" Award received from the Specialist School Trust.
2004	**22nd October**	Twin Grandchildren, Alexander George & Maria Diance Galanopoulos, born.
2004	**12th June**	Granted the O.B.E.
2004	**9th December**	Received the O.B.E. at Buckingham Palace.
2005	**February**	Acquired the RMI Consortium, consisting of five holiday resorts in the UK, Spain and Thailand.
2005	**March**	Awarded the "Silver Acorn" by the Scouts Association.
2005	**15th May**	Gt. Grandson, George Philip Bruce born.
2005	**11th Nov**	Gt. Grandson, Samuel James Bruce born.
2006		Awarded an Honorary Fellowship of the Queen Mary University, East London.
2006		The Petchey Academy, Hackney opened.

2007		The Petchey Academy open for business.
2008		Awarded an Honorary Fellowship of the University of East Anglia.
2008		Awarded the "Silver Wolf" by the Scouts Association.
2009		The Petchey Centre for Entrepreneurship opened at the University of East London.
2009		TS Jack Petchey named and launched.
2010		TS Jack Petchey operational.
2011		Son John diagnosed with Myelodyspaic Syndrome.
2011	*12th Feb*	Great Grand-daughter Freya Alexa May Rantell born.
2011	*July*	Son John received bone marrow transplant.
2012	*6th Nov*	Great Grand-daughter Miller Stephanie Rae Rantell born.
2012	*16th March*	Awarded the CBE.
2012		Sold Petchey Leisure to MGM India.
2013		Awarded the Dale Carnegie Leadership Award.

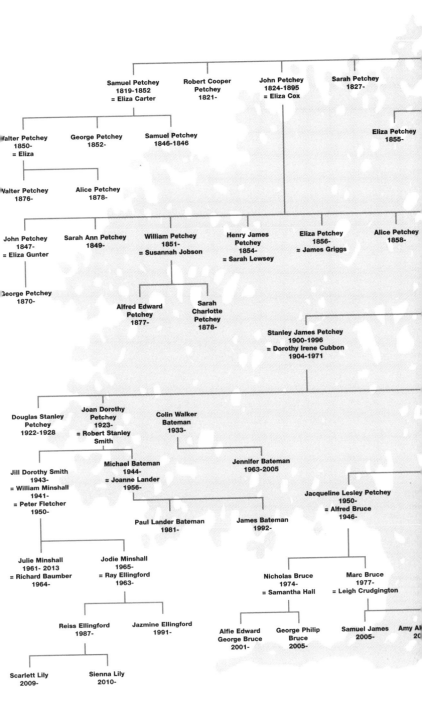

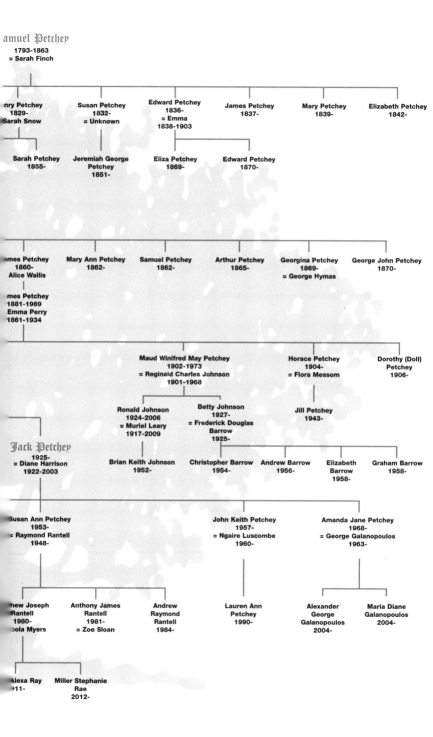

Samuel Petchey
1793-1863
= Sarah Finch

Henry Petchey
1829-
= Sarah Snow

Susan Petchey
1832-
= Unknown

Edward Petchey
1836-
= Emma
1838-1903

James Petchey
1837-

Mary Petchey
1839-

Elizabeth Petchey
1842-

Sarah Petchey
1855-

Jeremiah George Petchey
1851-

Eliza Petchey
1869-

Edward Petchey
1870-

James Petchey
1860-
= Alice Wallis

Mary Ann Petchey
1862-

Samuel Petchey
1862-

Arthur Petchey
1865-

Georgina Petchey
1869-
= George Hymas

George John Petchey
1870-

James Petchey
1881-1969
= Emma Perry
1861-1934

Maud Winifred May Petchey
1902-1973
= Reginald Charles Johnson
1901-1968

Horace Petchey
1904-
= Flora Messom

Dorothy (Doll) Petchey
1906-

Ronald Johnson
1924-2006
= Muriel Leary
1917-2009

Betty Johnson
1927-
= Frederick Douglas Barrow
1925-

Jill Petchey
1943-

Jack Petchey
1925-
= Diane Harrison
1922-2003

Brian Keith Johnson
1952-

Christopher Barrow
1954-

Andrew Barrow
1956-

Elizabeth Barrow
1958-

Graham Barrow
1958-

Susan Ann Petchey
1953-
= Raymond Rantell
1948-

John Keith Petchey
1957-
= Ngaire Luscombe
1960-

Amanda Jane Petchey
1968-
= George Galanopoulos
1963-

Matthew Joseph Rantell
1980-
= Nicola Myers

Anthony James Rantell
1981-
= Zoe Sloan

Andrew Raymond Rantell
1984-

Lauren Ann Petchey
1990-

Alexander George Galanopoulos
2004-

Maria Diane Galanopoulos
2004-

Alexa Ray
2011-

Miller Stephanie Rae
2012-

~ *INDEX* ~